BAKING

easy-to-make great home bakes

BAKING

easy-to-make great home bakes

contributing editor:
CAROLE CLEMENTS

HERMES
HOUSE

This edition published by Hermes House in 2002

© Anness Publishing Limited 1994, 1999, 2001

Hermes House is an imprint of
Anness Publishing Limited
Hermes House
88–89 Blackfriars Road
London SE1 8HA

A CIP catalogue record for this book is available from the British Library.

Publisher: Joanna Lorenz
Project Editor: Carole Clements
Designer: Sheila Volpe
Photography, styling: Amanda Heywood
Food Styling: Elizabeth Wolf-Cohen, Carla Capalbo,
steps by Cara Hobday, Teresa Goldfinch, Nicola Fowler

Front cover shows an adapted version of Cherry Strudel. For recipe see page 189.
Previously published as *The Great Big Baking Book*

3 5 7 9 10 8 6 4 2

NOTES
For all recipes, quantities are given in both metric and imperial measures and, where appropriate,
measures are also given in standard cups and spoons. Follow one set, but not a mixture, because they are
not interchangeable.
Standard spoon and cup measures are level.
1 tsp = 5ml, 1 tbsp = 15ml, 1 cup = 250ml/8fl oz
Australian standard tablespoons are 20ml. Australian readers should use 3 tsp in place of 1 tbsp for
measuring small quantities of gelatine, cornflour, salt, etc.
Medium eggs are used unless otherwise stated.

CONTENTS

~

INTRODUCTION

~

Nothing equals the satisfaction of home baking. No commercial cake mix or store-bought cookie can match one that is made from the best fresh ingredients with all the added enjoyment that baking at home provides – the enticing aromas that fill the house and stimulate appetites, the delicious straight-from-the-oven flavor, as well as the pride of having created such wonderful goodies yourself.

The Great American Baking Book is filled with familiar favorites from our melting-pot heritage, and many other less known, but equally good recipes. Explore the wealth of cookies, muffins, quick breads, yeast breads, pies, tarts, and cakes that await you within these pages. Even if you are a novice baker, the easy-to-follow and clear step-by-step photographs will help you achieve good results. For the more experienced home baker, this book will provide many recipes to add to your repertoire.

Baking is an exact science and needs to be approached in an ordered way. First read through the recipe from beginning to end. Set out all the required ingredients before you begin. In this book granulated sugar, all-purpose flour and size "large" eggs are assumed unless specified otherwise. Eggs should be at room temperature for best results. All the recipes use the scoop and then level method of measuring flour: scoop up flour with the measuring cup and level it off with the back of a knife. Sift the flour after you have measured it, and incorporate other dry ingredients as specified in the individual recipes. If you sift the flour from a fair height, it will have more chance to aerate and lighten.

When a recipe calls for folding one ingredient into another, it should be done in a way that incorporates as much air as possible into the batter. Use either a large metal spoon or a long rubber or plastic spatula. Gently plunge the spoon or spatula deep into the center of the batter and, scooping up a large amount of the batter, fold it over. Turn the bowl slightly so each scoop folds over another part of the batter.

No two ovens are alike. Buy a reliable oven thermometer and test the temperature of your oven. When possible bake in the center of the oven where the heat is more likely to be constant. If using a fan assisted oven, follow manufacturer's guidelines for baking. Good quality baking pans can improve your results, as they conduct heat more efficiently.

Practice, patience, and enthusiasm are the keys to confident and successful baking. *The Great American Baking Book* will inspire you to start sifting flour, breaking eggs and stirring up all sorts of delectable homemade treats – all guaranteed to bring great satisfaction to both the baker and those lucky enough to enjoy the results.

COOKIES & BARS

~

Keep the cookie jar filled with this wonderful array of cookies
and bars – some soft and chewy, some crunchy and nutty,
some rich and sinful, and some plain and wholesome.
All are irresistible.

Granola Cookies

MAKES 18

½ cup (1 stick) butter or margarine, at room temperature

½ cup light brown sugar, firmly packed

⅓ cup crunchy peanut butter

1 egg

½ cup flour

½ teaspoon baking powder

½ teaspoon cinnamon

⅛ teaspoon salt

2 cups granola cereal

⅓ cup raisins

½ cup walnuts, chopped

1 Preheat oven to 350°F. Grease a cookie sheet.

2 With an electric mixer, cream the butter or margarine and sugar until light and fluffy. Beat in the peanut butter. Beat in the egg.

3 ▲ Sift the flour, baking powder, cinnamon, and salt over the peanut butter mixture and stir to blend. Stir in the granola, raisins, and walnuts. Taste the mixture to see if it needs more sugar, as granolas vary.

4 ▲ Drop rounded tablespoonfuls of the batter onto the prepared cookie sheet about 1 inch apart. Press gently with the back of a spoon to spread each mound into a circle.

5 Bake until lightly colored, about 15 minutes. With a metal spatula, transfer to a rack to cool. Store in an airtight container.

Oatmeal and Cereal Cookies

MAKES 14

¾ cup (1½ sticks) butter or margarine, at room temperature

¾ cup sugar

1 egg yolk

1½ cups flour

1 teaspoon baking soda

½ teaspoon salt

½ cup rolled oats

½ cup small crunchy nugget cereal

> ### ~ VARIATION ~
>
> For Nutty Oatmeal Cookies, substitute an equal quantity of chopped walnuts or pecans for the cereal, and prepare as described.

1 ▲ With an electric mixer, cream the butter or margarine and sugar together until light and fluffy. Mix in the egg yolk.

2 Sift over the flour, baking soda, and salt, then stir into the butter mixture. Add the oats and cereal and stir to blend. Refrigerate for at least 20 minutes.

3 Preheat the oven to 375°F. Grease a cookie sheet.

4 ▲ Roll the dough into balls. Place them on the cookie sheet and flatten with the bottom of a floured glass.

5 Bake until golden, 10–12 minutes. With a metal spatula, transfer to a rack to cool completely. Store in an airtight container.

Granola Cookies (top), Oatmeal and Cereal Cookies

Coconut Oatmeal Cookies

MAKES 48

2 cups quick-cooking oats

1 cup shredded coconut

1 cup (2 sticks) butter or margarine, at room temperature

½ cup granulated sugar

¼ cup dark brown sugar, firmly packed

2 eggs

4 tablespoons milk

1½ teaspoons vanilla extract

1 cup flour

½ teaspoon baking soda

½ teaspoon salt

1 teaspoon ground cinnamon

1 Preheat the oven to 400°F. Lightly grease 2 cookie sheets.

2 ▲ Spread the oats and coconut on an ungreased baking sheet. Bake until golden brown, 8–10 minutes, stirring occasionally.

3 With an electric mixer, cream the butter or margarine and both sugars until light and fluffy. Beat in the eggs, 1 at a time, then the milk and vanilla. Sift over the dry ingredients and fold in. Stir in the oats and coconut.

4 ▼ Drop spoonfuls of the dough 1–2 inches apart on the prepared sheets and flatten with the bottom of a greased glass dipped in sugar. Bake until golden, 8–10 minutes. Transfer to a rack to cool.

Crunchy Jumbles

MAKES 36

½ cup (1 stick) butter or margarine, at room temperature

1 cup sugar

1 egg

1 teaspoon vanilla extract

1¼ cups flour

½ teaspoon baking soda

⅛ teaspooon salt

2 cups crisped rice cereal

1 cup chocolate chips

~ **VARIATION** ~

For even crunchier cookies, add ½ cup walnuts, coarsely chopped, with the cereal and chocolate chips.

1 Preheat the oven to 350°F. Lightly grease 2 cookie sheets.

2 ▲ With an electric mixer, cream the butter or margarine and sugar until light and fluffy. Beat in the egg and vanilla. Sift over the flour, baking soda, and salt and fold in.

3 ▼ Add the cereal and chocolate chips. Stir to mix thoroughly.

4 Drop the dough by spoonfuls 1–2 inches apart on the sheets. Bake until golden, 10–12 minutes. Transfer to a rack to cool.

Coconut Oatmeal Cookies (top), Crunchy Jumbles

Ginger Cookies

MAKES 36

1 cup granulated sugar

½ cup light brown sugar, firmly packed

½ cup (1 stick) butter, at room temperature

½ cup (1 stick) margarine, at room temperature

1 egg

⅓ cup molassses

2¼ cups flour

2 teaspoons ground ginger

½ teaspoon grated nutmeg

1 teaspoon ground cinnamon

2 teaspoons baking soda

½ teaspoon salt

1 Preheat the oven to 325°F. Line 2–3 cookie sheets with wax paper and grease lightly.

2 ▲ With an electric mixer, cream ½ cup of the granulated sugar, the brown sugar, butter, and margarine until light and fluffy. Add the egg and continue beating to blend well. Add the molasses.

3 ▲ Sift the dry ingredients 3 times, then stir into the butter mixture. Refrigerate for 30 minutes.

4 ▲ Place the remaining sugar in a shallow dish. Roll tablespoonfuls of the dough into balls, then roll the balls in the sugar to coat.

5 Place the balls 2 inches apart on the prepared sheets and flatten slightly. Bake until golden around the edges but soft in the middle, 12–15 minutes. Let stand for 5 minutes before transferring to a rack to cool.

> ### ~ VARIATION ~
>
> To make Gingerbread Men, increase the amount of flour by ¼ cup. Roll out the dough and cut out shapes with a special cutter. Decorate with icing, if wished.

Orange Cookies

MAKES 30

½ cup (1 stick) butter, at room temperature
1 cup sugar
2 egg yolks
1 tablespoon fresh orange juice
grated rind of 1 large orange
1 cup all-purpose flour
½ cup cake flour
½ teaspoon salt
1 teaspoon baking powder

1 ▲ With an electric mixer, cream the butter and sugar until light and fluffy. Add the yolks, orange juice and rind, and continue beating to blend. Set aside.

2 In another bowl, sift together the flours, salt, and baking powder. Add to the butter mixture and stir until it forms a dough.

3 ▲ Wrap the dough in wax paper and refrigerate for 2 hours.

4 Preheat the oven to 375°F. Grease 2 cookie sheets.

5 ▲ Roll spoonfuls of the dough into balls and place 1–2 inches apart on the prepared sheets.

6 ▼ Press down with a fork to flatten. Bake until golden brown, 8–10 minutes. With a metal spatula transfer to a rack to cool.

Snickerdoodles

MAKES 30

½ cup (1 stick) butter, at room
    temperature

1½ cups sugar

1 teaspoon vanilla extract

2 eggs

¼ cup milk

3½ cups flour

1 teaspoon baking soda

½ cup walnuts or pecans, finely
    chopped

FOR THE COATING

5 tablespoons sugar

2 tablespoons ground cinnamon

1 With an electric mixer, cream the
butter until light. Add the sugar and
vanilla and continue until fluffy. Beat
in the eggs, then the milk.

2 ▲ Sift the flour and baking soda
over the butter mixture and stir to
blend. Stir in the nuts. Refrigerate for
15 minutes. Preheat the oven to
375°F. Grease 2 cookie sheets.

3 ▲ For the coating, mix the sugar
and cinnamon. Roll tablespoonfuls of
the dough into walnut-size balls. Roll
the balls in the sugar mixture. You
may need to work in batches.

4 Place 2 inches apart on the
prepared sheets and flatten slightly.
Bake until golden, about 10 minutes.
Transfer to a rack to cool.

Chewy Chocolate Cookies

MAKES 18

4 egg whites

2½ cups confectioners' sugar

1 cup unsweetened cocoa powder

2 tablespoons flour

1 teaspoon instant coffee

1 tablespoon water

1 cup walnuts, finely chopped

1 Preheat the oven to 350°F. Line 2
cookie sheets with wax paper and
grease the paper.

2 With an electric mixer, beat the
egg whites until frothy.

3 ▼ Sift the sugar, cocoa, flour, and
coffee into the whites. Add the water
and continue beating on low speed to
blend, then on high for a few minutes
until the mixture thickens. With a
rubber spatula, fold in the walnuts.

4 ▲ Place generous spoonfuls of the
mixture 1 inch apart on the prepared
sheets. Bake until firm and cracked on
top but soft on the inside, 12–15
minutes. With a metal spatula,
transfer to a rack to cool.

> **~ VARIATION ~**
>
> If wished, add ½ cup chocolate
> chips to the dough with the nuts.

Snickerdoodles (top), Chewy Chocolate Cookies

Chocolate Pretzels

MAKES 28

1 cup flour

⅛ teaspoon salt

3 tablespoons unsweetened cocoa powder

½ cup (1 stick) butter, at room temperature

⅔ cup sugar

1 egg

1 egg white, lightly beaten, for glazing

sugar crystals, for sprinkling

1 Sift together the flour, salt and cocoa powder. Set aside. Grease 2 cookie sheets.

2 ▲ With an electric mixer, cream the butter until light. Add the sugar and continue beating until light and fluffy. Beat in the egg. Add the dry ingredients and stir to blend. Gather the dough into a ball, wrap in wax paper, and refrigerate for 1 hour or freeze for 30 minutes.

3 ▲ Roll the dough into 28 small balls. If the dough is sticky, flour your hands. Refrigerate the balls until needed. Preheat the oven to 375°F.

4 ▲ Roll each ball into a rope about 10 inches long. With each rope, form a loop with the two ends facing you. Twist the ends and fold back on to the circle, pressing in to make a pretzel shape. Place on the prepared sheets.

5 ▲ Brush the pretzels with the egg white. Sprinkle sugar crystals over the tops and bake until firm, 10–12 minutes. Transfer to a rack to cool.

Cream Cheese Spirals

MAKES 32

1 cup (2 sticks) butter, at room temperature
8 ounces cream cheese
2 teaspoons granulated sugar
2 cups flour
1 egg white beaten with 1 tablespoon water, for glazing
granulated sugar, for sprinkling
FOR THE FILLING
1 cup walnuts or pecans, finely chopped
½ cup light brown sugar, firmly packed
1 teaspoon ground cinnamon

1 With an electric mixer, cream the butter, cream cheese, and sugar until soft. Sift over the flour and mix to form a dough. Gather into a ball and divide in half. Flatten each half, wrap in wax paper and refrigerate for at least 30 minutes.

2 Meanwhile, make the filling. Mix together the chopped walnuts or pecans, the brown sugar, and the cinnamon. Set aside.

3 Preheat the oven to 375°F. Grease 2 cookie sheets.

4 ▲ Working with one half of the dough at a time, roll out thinly into a circle about 11 inches in diameter. Trim the edges with a knife, using a dinner plate as a guide.

5 ▼ Brush the surface with the egg white glaze and sprinkle the dough evenly with half the filling.

6 Cut the dough into quarters, and each quarter into 4 sections, to form 16 triangles.

7 ▲ Starting from the base of the triangles, roll up to form spirals.

8 Place on the sheets and brush with the remaining glaze. Sprinkle with granulated sugar. Bake until golden, 15–20 minutes. Cool on a rack.

Vanilla Crescents

MAKES 36

1¼ cups unblanched almonds

1 cup flour

½ teaspoon salt

1 cup (2 sticks) unsalted butter, at room temperature

½ cup granulated sugar

1 teaspoon vanilla extract

confectioners' sugar, for dusting

1 Grind the almonds with a few tablespoons of the flour in a food processor, blender, or nut grinder.

2 Sift the remaining flour with the salt. Set aside.

3 With an electric mixer, cream the butter and sugar together until light and fluffy.

4 ▼ Add the almonds, vanilla, and the flour mixture. Stir to mix well. Gather the dough into a ball, wrap in wax paper, and refrigerate for at least 30 minutes.

5 Preheat the oven to 325°F. Lightly grease 2 cookie sheets.

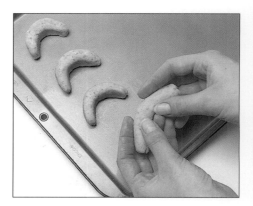

6 ▲ Break off walnut-size pieces of dough and roll into small cylinders about ½ inch in diameter. Bend into small crescents and place on the prepared cookie sheets.

7 Bake until dry but not brown, about 20 minutes. Transfer to a rack to cool only slightly. Set the rack over a baking sheet and dust with an even layer of confectioners' sugar.

Walnut Crescents

MAKES 72

1 cup walnuts

1 cup (2 sticks) unsalted butter, at room temperature

¾ cup granulated sugar

½ teaspoon vanilla extract

2 cups flour

¼ teaspoon salt

confectioners' sugar, for dusting

1 Preheat the oven to 350°F.

2 Grind the walnuts in a food processor, blender, or nut grinder until they are almost a paste. Transfer to a bowl.

3 Add the butter to the walnuts and mix with a wooden spoon until blended. Add the granulated sugar and vanilla and stir to blend.

4 ▼ Sift the flour and salt into the walnut mixture. Work into a dough with your hands.

5 Shape the dough, a teaspoonful at a time, into small cylinders about 1½ inches long. Bend into crescents and place evenly spaced on an ungreased cookie sheet.

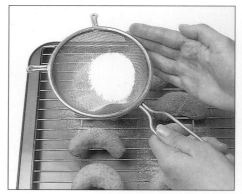

6 ▲ Bake until lightly browned, about 15 minutes. Transfer to a rack to cool only slightly. Set the rack over a baking sheet and dust lightly with confectioners' sugar.

Vanilla Crescents (top), Walnut Crescents

Pecan Puffs

MAKES 24

½ cup (1 stick) unsalted butter, at room
  temperature

2 tablespoons granulated sugar

⅛ teaspoon salt

1 teaspoon vanilla extract

1 cup pecans

1 cup sifted cake flour

confectioners' sugar, for dusting

1 Preheat the oven to 300°F. Grease
2 cookie sheets.

2 ▲ With an electric mixer, cream
the butter and sugar until light and
fluffy. Stir in the salt and vanilla.

3 Grind the nuts in a food processor,
blender, or nut grinder. Stir several
times to prevent the nuts becoming
oily. If necessary, grind in batches.

4 ▲ Force the ground nuts through a
strainer set over a bowl to aerate
them. Pieces too large to go through
the strainer can be ground again.

5 ▲ Sift the cake flour before
measuring. Stir the nuts and flour into
the butter mixture.

6 Roll the dough into marble-size
balls between the palms of your hands.
Place on the prepared sheets and bake
for 45 minutes.

7 ▲ While the puffs are still hot,
roll in confectioners' sugar. Let cool
completely, then roll once more in
confectioners' sugar.

Pecan Tassies

MAKES 24

4 ounces cream cheese
½ cup (1 stick) butter, at room temperature
1 cup flour
FOR THE FILLING
2 eggs
¾ cup dark brown sugar, firmly packed
1 teaspoon vanilla extract
⅛ teaspoon salt
2 tablespoons butter, melted
1 cup pecans

1 Place a baking sheet in the oven and preheat to 350°F. Grease 2 12-cup mini-muffin tins.

2 Cut the cream cheese and butter in pieces. Put in a mixing bowl. Sift over the flour and mix to form a dough.

3 ▲ Roll the dough out thinly. With a fluted pastry cutter, stamp out 24 2½-inch rounds. Line the muffin cups with the rounds and refrigerate while making the filling.

~ **VARIATION** ~

To make Jam Tassies, fill the cream cheese pastry shells with raspberry or blackberry jam, or other fruit jam. Bake as described.

4 For the filling, lightly whisk the eggs in a bowl. Gradually whisk in the brown sugar, a few tablespoons at a time, and add the vanilla, salt, and butter. Set aside.

5 ▼ Reserve 24 undamaged pecan halves and chop the rest coarsely with a sharp knife.

6 ▲ Place a spoonful of chopped nuts in each muffin cup and cover with the filling. Set a pecan half on the top of each.

7 Bake on the hot baking sheet until puffed and set, about 20 minutes. Transfer to a rack to cool. Serve at room temperature.

Lady Fingers

MAKES 24

²⁄₃ cup flour

¹⁄₈ teaspoon salt

4 eggs, separated

¹⁄₂ cup granulated sugar

¹⁄₂ teaspoon vanilla extract

confectioners' sugar, for sprinkling

1 Preheat the oven to 300°F. Grease 2 cookie sheets, then coat lightly with flour, and shake off the excess.

2 Sift the flour and salt twice.

> **~ COOK'S TIP ~**
>
> To make the cookies all the same length, mark parallel lines 4 inches apart on the greased cookie sheet, and pipe between the lines.

3 With an electric mixer, beat the egg yolks with half the sugar until thick enough to leave a ribbon trail when the beaters are lifted.

4 ▲ In another bowl, beat the egg whites until stiff. Beat in the remaining sugar until glossy.

5 Sift the flour over the yolks and spoon a large dollop of egg whites over the flour. Carefully fold in with a large metal spoon, adding the vanilla. Gently fold in the remaining whites.

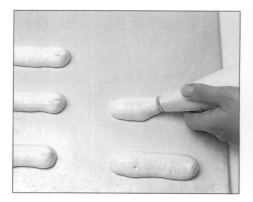

6 ▲ Spoon the mixture into a pastry bag fitted with a large plain nozzle. Pipe out 4-inch long lines on the prepared sheets about 1 inch apart. Sift over a layer of confectioners' sugar. Quickly turn the sheet upside down to dislodge any excess sugar.

7 Bake until crusty on the outside but soft in the center, about 20 minutes. Allow to cool slightly on the cookie sheet before transferring to a rack to cool completely.

Walnut Cookies

MAKES 60

¹⁄₂ cup (1 stick) butter or margarine, at room temperature

³⁄₄ cup sugar

1 cup flour

2 teaspoons vanilla extract

1 cup walnuts, finely chopped

> **~ VARIATION ~**
>
> To make Almond Cookies, use an equal amount of finely chopped unblanched almonds instead of walnuts. Replace half the vanilla with ¹⁄₂ teaspoon almond extract.

1 Preheat the oven to 300°F. Grease 2 cookie sheets.

2 ▲ With an electric mixer, cream the butter or margarine until soft. Add ¹⁄₃ cup of the sugar and continue beating until light and fluffy. Stir in the flour, vanilla, and walnuts.

3 Drop teaspoonfuls of the batter 1–2 inches apart on the sheets and flatten slightly with a fork. Bake until deep golden, about 25 minutes.

4 ▼ Transfer to a rack set over a baking sheet and sprinkle with the remaining sugar.

Lady Fingers (top), Walnut Cookies

Italian Almond Cookies

MAKES 48

1 cup unblanched almonds
1½ cups flour
½ cup sugar
⅛ teaspoon salt
⅛ teaspoon ground saffron
½ teaspoon baking soda
2 eggs
1 egg white, lightly beaten

~ COOK'S TIP ~

Serve these cookies after a meal, for dunking in glasses of sweet white wine, such as an Italian *Vin Santo* or a French *Muscat de Beaumes-de-Venise*.

1 Preheat the oven to 375°F. Grease and flour 2 cookie sheets.

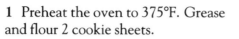

2 ▲ Spread the almonds in a baking tray and bake until lightly browned, about 15 minutes. When cool, grind ¼ cup of the almonds in a food processor, blender, or nut grinder until pulverized. Coarsely chop the remaining almonds in 2 or 3 pieces each. Set aside.

3 ▲ Combine the flour, sugar, salt, saffron, baking soda, and ground almonds in a bowl and mix to blend. Make a well in the center and add the 2 eggs. Stir from the center to form a rough dough. Transfer to a floured surface and knead until well blended. Knead in the chopped almonds.

4 ▲ Divide the dough into 3 equal parts. With your hands, roll into logs about 1 inch in diameter. Place on one of the prepared sheets; leave room for spreading. Brush with the egg white. Bake for 20 minutes.

5 ▲ Remove from the oven and lower the heat to 275°F. With a very sharp knife, cut at an angle into ½-inch slices. Return the slices to the oven and bake for 25 minutes more. Transfer to a rack to cool.

Christmas Cookies

MAKES 30

¾ cup (1½ sticks) unsalted butter, at room temperature

1¼ cups sugar

1 egg

1 egg yolk

1 teaspoon vanilla extract

grated rind of 1 lemon

¼ teaspoon salt

2½ cups flour

FOR DECORATING (OPTIONAL)

colored icing and small candies such as silver balls, red hots, colored sugar sprinkles, etc.

1 ▲ With an electric mixer, cream the butter until soft. Add the sugar gradually and continue beating until light and fluffy.

2 ▲ Using a wooden spoon, slowly mix in the whole egg and the egg yolk. Add the vanilla, lemon rind and salt. Stir to mix well.

3 Add the flour and stir to blend. Gather the dough into a ball, wrap, and refrigerate for 30 minutes.

4 ▼ Preheat the oven to 375°F. On a floured surface, roll out the dough about ⅛ inch thick.

5 ▲ Stamp out shapes or rounds with cookie cutters.

6 Bake until lightly colored, about 8 minutes. Transfer to a rack and let cool completely before decorating, if wished, with icing and candies.

Toasted Oat Meringues

MAKES 12

¾ cup old-fashioned oats

2 egg whites

⅛ teaspoon salt

1½ teaspoons cornstarch

¾ cup sugar

1 Preheat the oven to 275°F. Spread the oats in a baking tray and toast in the the oven until golden, about 10 minutes. Lower the heat to 250°F. Grease and flour a baking sheet.

~ **VARIATION** ~

Add ½ teaspoon ground cinnamon with the oats, and fold in gently.

2 ▼ With an electric mixer, beat the egg whites and salt until they start to form soft peaks.

3 Sift over the cornstarch and continue beating until the whites hold stiff peaks. Add half the sugar and whisk until glossy.

4 ▲ Add the remaining sugar and fold in, then fold in the oats.

5 Gently spoon the mixture onto the prepared sheet and bake for 2 hours.

6 When done, turn off the oven. Lift the meringues from the tray, turn over, and set in another place on the sheet to prevent sticking. Leave in the oven as it cools down.

Meringues

MAKES 24

4 egg whites

⅛ teaspoon salt

1¼ cups sugar

½ teaspoon vanilla or almond extract (optional)

1 cup whipped cream (optional)

1 Preheat the oven to 225°F. Grease and flour 2 large cookie sheets.

2 With an electric mixer, beat the egg whites and salt in a very clean metal bowl on low speed. When they start to form soft peaks, add half the sugar and continue beating until the mixture holds stiff peaks.

3 ▲ With a large metal spoon, fold in the remaining sugar and vanilla or almond extract, if using.

4 ▼ Pipe the meringue mixture or gently spoon it on the prepared sheet.

5 Bake for 2 hours. Turn off the oven. Loosen the meringues, invert, and set in another place on the sheets to prevent sticking. Leave in the oven as it cools. Serve sandwiched with whipped cream, if desired.

Toasted Oat Meringues (top), Meringues

Chocolate Macaroons

MAKES 24

2 1-ounce squares unsweetened chocolate

1 cup blanched almonds

1 cup granulated sugar

⅓ cup egg whites (about 3 eggs)

½ teaspoon vanilla extract

¼ teaspoon almond extract

confectioners' sugar, for dusting

1 Preheat the oven to 325°F. Line 2 cookie sheets with wax paper and grease the paper.

2 ▼ Melt the chocolate in the top of a double boiler, or in a heatproof bowl set over a pan of hot water.

3 ▲ Grind the almonds finely in a food processor, blender, or nut grinder. Transfer to a mixing bowl.

4 ▲ Add the sugar, egg whites, vanilla, and almond extract and stir to blend. Stir in the chocolate. The mixture should just hold its shape. If it is too soft, refrigerate for 15 minutes.

5 ▲ Use a teaspoon and your hands to shape the dough into walnut-size balls. Place on the sheets and flatten slightly. Brush each ball with a little water and sift over a thin layer of confectioners' sugar. Bake until just firm, 10–12 minutes. With a metal spatula, transfer to a rack to cool.

~ **VARIATION** ~

For Chocolate Pine Nut Macaroons, spread ¾ cup pine nuts in a shallow dish. Press the balls of chocolate macaroon dough into the nuts to cover one side and bake as described, nut-side up.

Coconut Macaroons

MAKES 24

⅓ cup flour

⅛ teaspoon salt

2½ cups shredded coconut

⅔ cup sweetened condensed milk

1 teaspoon vanilla extract

1 Preheat the oven to 350°F. Grease 2 cookie sheets.

2 Sift the flour and salt into a bowl. Stir in the coconut.

3 ▲ Pour in the milk. Add the vanilla and stir from the center to make a very thick batter.

4 ▼ Drop heaped tablespoonfuls of batter 1 inch apart on prepared sheets. Bake until golden brown, about 20 minutes. Cool on a rack.

Chocolate Macaroons (top), Coconut Macaroons

Almond Tiles

MAKES 40

½ cup blanched almonds

½ cup sugar

3½ tablespoons unsalted butter

2 egg whites

⅓ cup cake flour

½ teaspoon vanilla extract

1 cup sliced almonds

1 Grind the blanched almonds with 2 tablespoons of the sugar in a food processor, blender, or nut grinder.

2 Preheat the oven to 425°F. Grease 2 cookie sheets.

3 ▲ With an electric mixer, cream the butter and remaining sugar together until light and fluffy.

4 Add the egg whites and stir until just blended. Sift over the flour and fold in with a metal spoon. Fold in the ground almonds and vanilla.

5 ▲ Working in small batches, drop tablespoonfuls of the batter 3 inches apart on one of the prepared sheets. With the back of a spoon, spread out into thin, almost transparent circles about 2½ inches in diameter. Sprinkle each circle with some of the sliced almonds.

6 Bake until the outer edges have browned slightly, about 4 minutes.

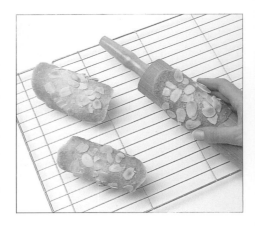

7 ▲ Remove from the oven. With a metal spatula, quickly transfer the cookies to a rolling pin to form a curved shape. Transfer to a rack when firm. If the cookies harden too quickly to shape, reheat briefly. Repeat the baking and shaping process until the batter is used up. Store the cookies in an airtight container.

Florentines

MAKES 36

3 tablespoons butter

½ cup whipping cream

⅔ cup sugar

1½ cups sliced almonds

¼ cup candied orange peel, finely chopped

2 tablespoons chopped candied cherries

½ cup flour, sifted

8 1-ounce squares semisweet chocolate

1 teaspoon vegetable oil

1 Preheat the oven to 350°F. Grease 2 cookie sheets.

2 ▲ Melt the butter, cream, and sugar together and slowly bring to the boil. Take off the heat and stir in the almonds, orange peel, cherries, and flour until blended.

3 Drop teaspoonfuls of the batter 1–2 inches apart on the prepared sheets and flatten with a fork.

4 Bake until the cookies brown at the edges, about 10 minutes. Remove from the oven and correct the shape by quickly pushing in any thin uneven edges with a knife or a round cookie cutter. Work fast or they will cool and harden while still on the sheets. If necessary, return to the oven for a few moments to soften. While still hot, use a metal spatula to transfer the cookies to a clean, flat surface.

5 Melt the chocolate in the top of a double boiler or in a heatproof bowl set over a pan of hot water. Add the oil and stir to blend.

6 ▲ With a metal spatula, spread the smooth underside of the cooled cookies with a thin coating of the melted chocolate.

7 ▼ When the chocolate is about to set, draw a serrated knife across the surface with a slight sawing motion to make wavy lines. Store in an airtight container in a cool place.

Nut Lace Cookies

MAKES 18

½ cup blanched almonds

4 tablespoons butter

3 tablespoons flour

½ cup sugar

2 tablespoons heavy cream

½ teaspoon vanilla extract

1 Preheat the oven to 375°F. Grease 1–2 cookie sheets.

2 With a sharp knife, chop the almonds as finely as possible. Alternatively, use a food processor, blender, or nut grinder to chop the nuts very finely.

3 ▼ Melt the butter in a saucepan over low heat. Remove from the heat and stir in the remaining ingredients and the almonds.

4 Drop teaspoonfuls 2½ inches apart on the prepared sheets. Bake until golden, about 5 minutes. Cool on the sheets briefly, just until the cookies are stiff enough to lift off.

5 ▲ With a metal spatula, transfer to a rack to cool completely.

~ **VARIATION** ~

Add ¼ cup finely chopped candied orange peel to the batter.

Oatmeal Lace Cookies

MAKES 36

⅔ cup (10⅔ tablespoons) butter or margarine

1½ cups rolled oats

¾ cup dark brown sugar, firmly packed

¾ cup granulated sugar

3 tablespoons flour

¼ teaspoon salt

1 egg, lightly beaten

1 teaspoon vanilla extract

½ cup pecans or walnuts, finely chopped

1 Preheat the oven to 350°F. Grease 2 cookie sheets.

2 Melt the butter or margarine in a saucepan over low heat. Set aside.

3 In a mixing bowl, combine the oats, brown sugar, granulated sugar, flour, and salt.

4 ▲ Make a well in the center and add the butter or margarine, the egg, and vanilla.

5 ▼ Mix until blended, then stir in the chopped nuts.

6 Drop rounded teaspoonfuls of the batter about 2 inches apart on the prepared sheets. Bake until lightly browned on the edges and bubbling, 5–8 minutes. Let cool on the sheet for 2 minutes, then transfer to a rack to cool completely.

Nut Lace Cookies (top), Oatmeal Lace Cookies

Raspberry Sandwich Cookies

MAKES 32

1 cup blanched almonds

1½ cups flour

¾ cup (1½ sticks) butter, at room temperature

½ cup sugar

grated rind of 1 lemon

1 teaspoon vanilla extract

1 egg white

⅛ teaspoon salt

⅓ cup slivered almonds

1 cup raspberry jam

1 tablespoon fresh lemon juice

1 Place the blanched almonds and 3 tablespoons of the flour in a food processor, blender, or nut grinder and process until finely ground. Set aside.

2 With an electric mixer, cream the butter and sugar together until light and fluffy. Stir in the lemon rind and vanilla. Add the ground almonds and remaining flour and mix well to form a dough. Gather into a ball, wrap in wax paper, and refrigerate for at least 1 hour.

3 Preheat oven to 325°F. Line 2 cookie sheets with wax paper.

4 Divide the dough into 4 equal parts. Working with one section of the dough at a time, roll out to a thickness of ⅛ inch on a lightly floured surface. With a 2½-inch fluted pastry cutter, stamp out circles. Gather the dough scraps, roll out, and stamp out more circles. Repeat with the remaining dough.

5 ▲ With the small end of a piping tip, or with a ¾-inch cutter, stamp out the centers from half the circles. Place dough rings and circles ½ inch apart on the prepared sheets.

6 ▲ Whisk the egg white with the salt until just frothy. Chop the slivered almonds. Brush only the cookie rings with the egg white, then sprinkle over the almonds. Bake until very lightly browned, 12–15 minutes. Let cool for a few minutes on the sheets before transferring to a rack.

7 ▲ In a saucepan, melt the jam with the lemon juice until it comes to a simmer. Brush the jam over the cookie circles and sandwich together with the rings. Store in an airtight container with sheets of wax paper between the layers.

Brandy Snaps

MAKES 18

4 tablespoons butter, at room temperature
⅔ cup sugar
1 rounded tablespoon corn syrup
⅓ cup flour
½ teaspoon ground ginger
FOR THE FILLING
1 cup whipping cream
2 tablespoons brandy

1 With an electric mixer, cream together the butter and sugar until light and fluffy, then beat in the corn syrup. Sift over the flour and ginger and mix to a rough dough.

2 ▲ Transfer the dough to a work surface and knead until smooth. Cover and refrigerate for 30 minutes.

3 Preheat the oven to 375°F. Grease a cookie sheet.

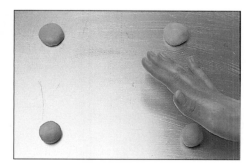

4 ▲ Working in batches of 4, form walnut-size balls of dough. Place far apart on the prepared sheet and flatten slightly. Bake until golden and bubbling, about 10 minutes.

5 ▼ Remove from the oven and let cool a few moments. Working quickly, slide a metal spatula under each one, turn over, and wrap around the handle of a wooden spoon (have four spoons ready). If they firm up too quickly, reheat for a few seconds to soften. When firm, slide the snaps off and place on a rack to cool.

6 ▲ When all the brandy snaps are cool, prepare the filling. Whip the cream and brandy until soft peaks form. Fill a pastry bag with the brandy cream. Pipe into each end of the brandy snaps just before serving.

Shortbread

MAKES 8

⅔ cup (10⅔ tablespoons) unsalted butter, at room temperature

½ cup sugar

1¼ cups all-purpose flour

½ cup rice flour

¼ teaspoon baking powder

⅛ teaspoon salt

1 Preheat the oven to 325°F. Grease a shallow 8-inch cake pan.

2 With an electric mixer, cream the butter and sugar together until light and fluffy. Sift over the flours, baking powder, and salt and mix well.

3 ▲ Press the dough neatly into the prepared pan, smoothing the surface with the back of a spoon.

4 Prick all over with a fork, then score into 8 equal wedges.

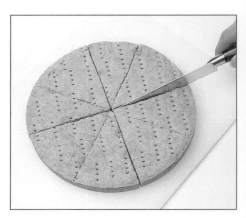

5 ▲ Bake until golden, 40–45 minutes. Leave in the pan until cool enough to handle, then unmold and recut the wedges while still hot. Store in an airtight container.

Oatmeal Wedges

MAKES 8

4 tablespoons butter

1 rounded tablespoon dark corn syrup

⅓ cup dark brown sugar, firmly packed

1¼ cups quick-cooking oats

⅛ teaspoon salt

1 ▲ Preheat the oven to 350°F. Line an 8-inch shallow cake pan with wax paper and grease the paper.

2 ▼ Place the butter, corn syrup, and sugar in a pan over low heat. Cook, stirring, until melted and combined.

~ **VARIATION** ~

If wished, add 1 teaspoon ground ginger to the melted butter.

3 ▲ Remove from the heat and add the oats and salt. Stir to blend.

4 Spoon into the prepared pan and smooth the surface. Place in the center of the oven and bake until golden brown, 20–25 minutes. Leave in the pan until cool enough to handle, then unmold and cut into wedges while still hot.

Shortbread (top), Oatmeal Wedges

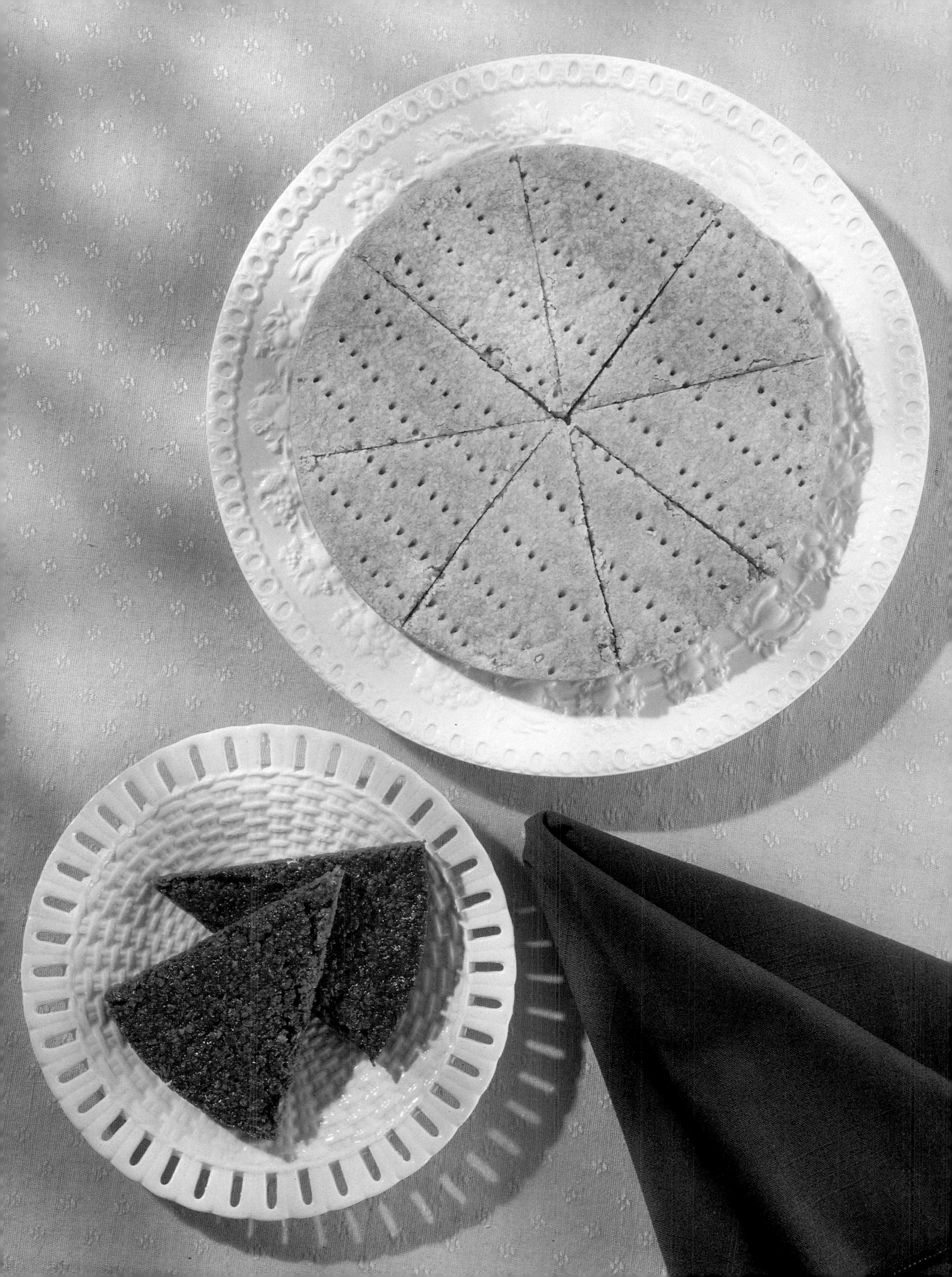

Chocolate-Nut Refrigerator Cookies

MAKES 50

1 1-ounce square semisweet chocolate
1 1-ounce square unsweetened chocolate
2 cups flour
½ teaspoon salt
1 cup (2 sticks) unsalted butter, at room temperature
1 cup sugar
2 eggs
1 teaspoon vanilla extract
1 cup walnuts, finely chopped

1 Melt the chocolates in the top of a double boiler, or in a heatproof bowl set over a pan of gently simmering water. Set aside.

2 ▼ In a small bowl, sift together the flour and salt. Set aside.

3 With an electric mixer, cream the butter until soft. Add the sugar and continue beating until the mixture is light and fluffy.

4 Mix the eggs and vanilla, then gradually stir into the butter mixture.

5 ▲ Stir in the chocolate, then the flour. Stir in the nuts.

6 ▲ Divide the dough into 4 parts, and roll each into 2-inch diameter logs. Wrap tightly in foil and refrigerate or freeze until firm.

7 Preheat the oven to 375°F. Grease 2 cookie sheets.

8 With a sharp knife, cut the dough into ¼-inch slices. Place the rounds on the prepared sheets and bake until lightly colored, about 10 minutes. Transfer to a rack to cool.

~ **VARIATION** ~

For two-tone cookies, melt only 1 ounce of chocolate. Combine all the ingredients, except the chocolate, as above. Divide the dough in half. Add the chocolate to one half. Roll out the plain dough to a flat sheet. Roll out the chocolate dough, place on top of the plain dough and roll up. Wrap, slice and bake as described.

Cinnamon Refrigerator Cookies

MAKES 50

2⅛ cups flour

½ teaspoon salt

2 teaspoons ground cinnamon

1 cup (2 sticks) unsalted butter, at room temperature

1 cup sugar

2 eggs

1 teaspoon vanilla extract

1 In a bowl, sift together the flour, salt, and cinnamon. Set aside.

2 ▲ With an electric mixer, cream the butter until soft. Add the sugar and continue beating until the mixture is light and fluffy.

3 Beat the eggs and vanilla, then gradually stir into the butter mixture.

4 ▲ Stir in the dry ingredients.

5 ▲ Divide the dough into 4 parts, then roll each into 2-inch diameter logs. Wrap tightly in foil and refrigerate or freeze until firm.

6 Preheat the oven to 375°F. Grease 2 cookie sheets.

7 ▼ With a sharp knife, cut the dough into ¼-inch slices. Place the rounds on the prepared sheets and bake until lightly colored, about 10 minutes. With a metal spatula, transfer to a rack to cool.

Peanut Butter Cookies

MAKES 24

1 cup flour

½ teaspoon baking soda

½ teaspoon salt

½ cup (1 stick) butter, at room
    temperature

¾ cup light brown sugar, firmly packed

1 egg

1 teaspoon vanilla extract

1 cup crunchy peanut butter

1 Sift together the flour, baking soda,
and salt and set aside.

2 With an electric mixer, cream the
butter and sugar together until light
and fluffy.

3 In another bowl, mix the egg and
vanilla, then gradually beat into the
butter mixture.

4 ▲ Stir in the peanut butter and
blend thoroughly. Stir in the dry
ingredients. Refrigerate for at least
30 minutes, or until firm.

5 Preheat the oven to 350°F. Grease
2 cookie sheets.

6 Spoon out rounded teaspoonfuls of
the dough and roll into balls.

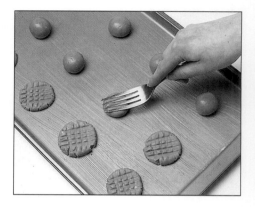

7 ▲ Place the balls on the prepared
sheets and press flat with a fork into
circles about 2½ inches in diameter,
making a criss-cross pattern. Bake
until lightly colored, 12–15 minutes.
Transfer to a rack to cool.

~ **VARIATION** ~

Add ½ cup peanuts, coarsely
chopped, with the peanut butter.

Tollhouse Cookies

MAKES 24

½ cup (1 stick) butter or margarine, at
    room temperature

¼ cup granulated sugar

½ cup dark brown sugar, firmly packed

1 egg

½ teaspoon vanilla extract

1⅛ cup flour

½ teaspoon baking soda

⅛ teaspoon salt

1 cup chocolate chips

½ cup walnuts, chopped

1 Preheat the oven to 350°F. Grease
2 large cookie sheets.

2 ▼ With an electric mixer, cream
the butter or margarine and two sugars
together until light and fluffy.

3 In another bowl, mix the egg and
vanilla, then gradually beat into the
butter mixture. Sift over the flour,
baking soda, and salt. Stir to blend.

4 ▲ Add the chocolate chips and
walnuts, and mix to combine well.

5 Place heaped teaspoonfuls of the
dough 2 inches apart on the prepared
sheets. Bake until lightly colored,
10–15 minutes. With a metal spatula,
transfer to a rack to cool.

Peanut Butter Cookies (top), Tollhouse Cookies

Salted Peanut Cookies

MAKES 70

3 cups flour

½ teaspoon baking soda

½ cup (1 stick) butter, at room
    temperature

½ cup (1 stick) margarine, at room
    temperature

1½ cups light brown sugar, firmly
    packed

2 eggs

2 teaspoons vanilla extract

2 cups salted peanuts

1 Preheat the oven to 375°F. Lightly
grease 2 cookie sheets.

2 Sift together the flour and baking
soda. Set aside.

3 ▲ With an electric mixer, cream
the butter, margarine, and sugar until
light and fluffy. Beat in the eggs and
vanilla. Fold in the flour mixture.

4 ▲ Stir in the peanuts.

5 ▲ Drop teaspoonfuls 2 inches apart
on the sheets. Flatten with the greased
bottom of a glass dipped in sugar.

6 Bake until lightly colored, about 10
minutes. With a metal spatula,
transfer to a rack to cool.

> **~ VARIATION ~**
>
> To make Cashew Cookies, substitute
> an equal amount of salted cashews
> for the peanuts, and add as above.
> The flavor is subtle and interesting.

Cheddar Pennies

MAKES 20

4 tablespoons butter, at room
    temperature

1 cup freshly grated cheddar cheese

⅓ cup flour

⅛ teaspoon salt

⅛–¼ teaspoon chili powder

1 With an electric mixer, cream the
butter until soft.

2 ▲ Stir in the cheese, flour, salt,
and chili. Gather to form a dough.

3 Transfer to a lightly floured surface.
Shape into a cylinder about 1¼
inches in diameter. Wrap in wax
paper and refrigerate for 1–2 hours.

4 Preheat the oven to 350°F. Grease
1–2 cookie sheets.

5 ▲ Slice the dough into ¼-inch
thick rounds and place on the sheets.
Bake until golden, about 15 minutes.
Transfer to a rack to cool.

Salted Peanut Cookies (top), Cheddar Pennies

Chocolate Chip Brownies

MAKES 24

4 1-ounce squares unsweetened chocolate

½ cup (1 stick) butter

3 eggs

1½ cups sugar

1 teaspoon vanilla extract

pinch of salt

¾ cup flour

1 cup chocolate chips

1 ▼ Preheat the oven to 350°F. Line the bottom and sides of a 13- × 9-inch pan with wax paper and grease.

2 ▲ Melt the chocolate and butter in the top of a double boiler, or in a heatproof bowl set over a pan of gently simmering water.

3 ▲ Beat together the eggs, sugar, vanilla, and salt. Stir in the chocolate mixture. Sift over the flour and fold in. Add the chocolate chips.

4 ▲ Pour the batter into the prepared pan and spread evenly. Bake until just set, about 30 minutes. Do not overbake; the brownies should be slightly moist inside. Cool in the pan.

5 To unmold, run a knife all around the edge and invert onto a cookie sheet. Remove the paper. Place another sheet on top and invert again so the brownies are right-side up. Cut into squares for serving.

Marbled Brownies

MAKES 24

8 1-ounce squares semisweet chocolate
6 tablespoons butter
4 eggs
1½ cups sugar
1 cup flour
½ teaspoon salt
1 teaspoon baking powder
2 teaspoons vanilla extract
l cup walnuts, chopped
FOR THE PLAIN BATTER
4 tablespoons butter, at room temperature
6 ounces cream cheese
½ cup sugar
2 eggs
2 tablespoons flour
1 teaspoon vanilla extract

1 Preheat the oven to 350°F. Line the bottom and sides of a 13- × 9-inch pan with wax paper and grease.

2 Melt the chocolate and butter over very low heat, stirring constantly. Set aside to cool.

3 Meanwhile, beat the eggs until light and fluffy. Gradually add the sugar and continue beating until blended. Sift over the flour, salt, and baking powder and fold to combine.

4 ▲ Stir in the cooled chocolate mixture. Add the vanilla and walnuts. Measure and set aside 2 cups of the chocolate batter.

5 ▲ For the plain batter, cream the butter and cream cheese with an electric mixer.

6 Add the sugar and continue beating until blended. Beat in the eggs, flour, and vanilla.

7 Spread the unmeasured chocolate batter in pan. Pour over the cream cheese mixture. Drop spoonfuls of the reserved chocolate batter on top.

8 ▲ With a metal spatula, swirl the mixtures to marble. Do not blend completely. Bake until just set, 35–40 minutes. Unmold when cool and cut into squares for serving.

Chocolate Pecan Squares

MAKES 16

2 eggs

2 teaspoons vanilla extract

⅛ teaspoon salt

1½ cups pecans, coarsely chopped

½ cup flour

¼ cup sugar

½ cup dark corn syrup

3 1-ounce squares semisweet chocolate, finely chopped

3 tablespoons butter

16 pecan halves, for decorating

1 Preheat the oven to 325°F. Line the bottom and sides of an 8-inch square baking pan with wax paper and grease lightly.

2 ▼ Whisk together the eggs, vanilla, and salt. In another bowl, mix together the pecans and flour. Set both aside.

3 In a saucepan, bring the sugar and corn syrup to a boil. Remove from the heat and stir in the chocolate and butter to blend thoroughly with a wooden spoon.

4 ▲ Mix in the beaten eggs, then fold in the pecan mixture.

5 Pour the batter into the prepared pan and bake until set, about 35 minutes. Cool in the pan for 10 minutes before unmolding. Cut into 2-inch squares and press pecan halves into the tops while warm. Cool completely on a rack.

Raisin Brownies

MAKES 16

½ cup (1 stick) butter or margarine

½ cup unsweetened cocoa powder

2 eggs

1 cup sugar

1 teaspoon vanilla extract

⅓ cup flour

¾ cup walnuts, chopped

½ cup raisins

1 Preheat the oven to 350°F. Line the bottom and sides of an 8-inch square baking pan and grease.

2 ▼ Gently melt the butter or margarine in a small saucepan. Remove from the heat and stir in the cocoa powder.

3 With an electric mixer, beat the eggs, sugar, and vanilla together until light. Add the cocoa mixture and stir to blend.

4 ▲ Sift the flour over the cocoa mixture and gently fold in. Add the walnuts and raisins and scrape the batter into the prepared pan.

5 Bake in the center of the oven for 30 minutes. Do not overbake. Leave in the pan to cool before cutting into 2-inch squares and removing. The brownies should be soft and moist.

Chocolate Pecan Squares (top), Raisin Brownies

Chocolate Walnut Bars

MAKES 24

½ cup walnuts

⅓ cup granulated sugar

¾ cup flour, sifted

6 tablespoons cold unsalted butter, cut in pieces

FOR THE TOPPING

2 tablespoons unsalted butter

⅓ cup water

⅓ cup unsweetened cocoa powder

½ cup granulated sugar

1 teaspoon vanilla extract

⅛ teaspoon salt

2 eggs

confectioners' sugar, for dusting

1 Preheat the oven to 350°F. Grease the sides and bottom of an 8-inch square baking pan.

2 ▼ Grind the walnuts with a few tablespoons of the sugar in a food processor, blender, or nut grinder.

3 In a bowl, combine the ground walnuts, remaining sugar, and flour. With a pastry blender, cut in the butter until the mixture resembles coarse crumbs. Alternatively, combine all the ingredients in a food processor and process until the mixture resembles coarse crumbs.

4 ▲ Pat the walnut mixture into the bottom of the prepared pan in an even layer. Bake for 25 minutes.

5 ▲ Meanwhile, for the topping, melt the butter with the water. Whisk in the cocoa and sugar. Remove the pan from the heat, stir in the vanilla and salt and let cool for 5 minutes. Whisk in the eggs until blended.

6 ▲ Pour the topping over the crust when baked.

7 Return to the oven and bake until set, about 20 minutes. Set the pan on a rack to cool. Cut into 2½- × 1-inch bars and dust with confectioners' sugar. Store in the refrigerator.

Pecan Bars

MAKES 36

2 cups flour
pinch of salt
½ cup granulated sugar
1 cup (2 sticks) cold butter or margarine, cut in pieces
1 egg
finely grated rind of 1 lemon
FOR THE TOPPING
¾ cup (1½ sticks) butter
¼ cup honey
¼ cup granulated sugar
¾ cup dark brown sugar, firmly packed
5 tablespoons whipping cream
4 cups pecan halves

1 Preheat the oven to 375°F. Lightly grease a 15½- × 10½- × 1-inch jelly roll pan.

2 ▲ For the crust, sift the flour and salt into a mixing bowl. Stir in the sugar. With a pastry blender, cut in the butter or margarine until the mixture resembles coarse crumbs. Add the egg and lemon rind and blend with a fork until the mixture just holds together.

3 ▼ Spoon the mixture into the prepared pan. With floured fingertips, press into an even layer. Prick the pastry all over with a fork and refrigerate for 10 minutes.

4 Bake the pastry crust for 15 minutes. Remove the pan from the oven, but keep the oven on while making the topping.

5 ▲ Melt the butter, honey, and both sugars. Bring to a boil. Boil, without stirring, for 2 minutes. Off the heat, stir in the cream and pecans. Pour over the crust, return to the oven and bake for 25 minutes.

6 When cool, run a knife around the edge. Invert onto a baking sheet, place another sheet on top and invert again. Dip a sharp knife into very hot water and cut into squares for serving.

Fig Bars

MAKES 48

2 cups dried figs

3 eggs

¾ cup granulated sugar

¾ cup flour

1 teaspoon baking powder

½ teaspoon ground cinnamon

¼ teaspoon ground cloves

¼ teaspoon grated nutmeg

¼ teaspoon salt

¾ cup walnuts, finely chopped

2 tablespoons brandy or cognac

confectioners' sugar, for dusting

1 Preheat the oven to 325°F. Line a 12- × 8- × 1½-inch pan with wax paper and grease.

2 ▲ With a sharp knife, chop the figs roughly. Set aside.

3 In a bowl, whisk the eggs and sugar until well blended. In another bowl, sift together the dry ingredients, then fold into the egg mixture in several batches.

4 ▼ Stir in the figs, walnuts, and brandy or cognac.

5 Scrape the mixture into the prepared pan and bake until the top is firm and brown, 35–40 minutes. It should still be soft underneath.

6 Let cool in the pan for 5 minutes, then unmold and transfer to a sheet of wax paper lightly sprinkled with confectioners' sugar. Cut into bars.

Lemon Bars

MAKES 36

½ cup confectioners' sugar

1½ cups flour

½ teaspoon salt

¾ cup (1½ sticks) butter, cut in small
  pieces

FOR THE TOPPING

4 eggs

1½ cups granulated sugar

grated rind of 1 lemon

½ cup fresh lemon juice

¾ cup whipping cream

confectioners' sugar, for dusting

1 Preheat the oven to 325°F. Grease a 13- × 9-inch baking pan.

2 Sift the sugar, flour, and salt into a bowl. With a pastry blender, cut in the butter until the mixture resembles coarse crumbs.

3 ▲ Press the mixture into the bottom of the prepared pan. Bake until golden brown, about 20 minutes.

4 Meanwhile, for the topping, whisk the eggs and sugar together until blended. Add the lemon rind and juice and mix well.

5 ▲ Lightly whip the cream and fold into the egg mixture. Pour over the still warm crust, return to the oven, and bake until set, about 40 minutes.

6 Cool completely before cutting into bars. Dust with confectioners' sugar.

Fig Bars (top), Lemon Bars

Apricot Bars

MAKES 12

½ cup light brown sugar, firmly packed

¾ cup flour

6 tablespoons cold unsalted butter, cut in pieces

FOR THE TOPPING

1 cup dried apricots

1 cup water

grated rind of 1 lemon

⅓ cup granulated sugar

2 teaspoons cornstarch

½ cup walnuts, chopped

1 Preheat the oven to 350°F.

2 ▲ In a bowl, combine the brown sugar and flour. With a pastry blender, cut in the butter until the mixture resembles coarse crumbs.

3 ▲ Transfer to an 8-inch square baking pan and press into an even layer. Bake for 15 minutes. Remove from the oven but leave the oven on.

4 Meanwhile, for the topping, combine the apricots and water in a saucepan and simmer until soft, about 10 minutes. Strain the liquid and reserve. Chop the apricots.

5 ▲ Return the apricots to the saucepan and add the lemon rind, granulated sugar, cornstarch, and 4 tablespoons of the soaking liquid. Cook for 1 minute.

6 ▲ Cool slightly before spreading the topping over the base. Sprinkle over the walnuts and continue baking for 20 minutes more. Let cool in the pan before cutting into bars.

Almond Bars

MAKES 36

6 tablespoons butter, at room temperature
¼ cup sugar
1 egg yolk
grated rind and juice of ½ lemon
½ teaspoon vanilla extract
2 tablespoons whipping cream
1 cup flour
FOR THE TOPPING
1 cup sugar
¾ cup sliced almonds
4 egg whites
½ teaspoon ground ginger
½ teaspoon ground cinnamon

4 With lightly floured fingers, press the dough into the pan in a thin even layer. Bake for 15 minutes. Remove from the oven but leave the oven on.

5 ▲ For the topping, combine all the ingredients in a heavy saucepan. Cook, stirring constantly, until the mixture comes to a boil.

6 Continue boiling until just golden, about 1 minute. Pour it over the dough, spreading it evenly.

7 ▲ Return to the oven and bake until golden, about 45 minutes. Remove and score into bars. Cool completely before cutting and serving.

1 ▲ Preheat the oven to 375°F. Line a 13- × 9-inch jelly-roll pan with wax paper and grease.

2 With an electric mixer, cream the butter and sugar until light and fluffy. Beat in the egg yolk, lemon rind and juice, vanilla and cream.

3 ▲ Gradually stir in the flour until mixed. Gather into a ball of dough.

Hermits

MAKES 30

¾ cup flour

1½ teaspoons baking powder

1 teaspoon ground cinnamon

½ teaspoon grated nutmeg

¼ teaspoon ground cloves

¼ teaspoon ground allspice

1½ cup raisins

½ cup (1 stick) butter or margarine, at
    room temperature

½ cup sugar

2 eggs

½ cup molasses

½ cup walnuts, chopped

1 Preheat the oven to 350°F. Line the bottom and sides of a 13- × 9-inch pan with wax paper and grease.

2 Sift together the flour, baking powder, and spices.

3 ▲ Place the raisins in another bowl and toss with a few tablespoons of the flour mixture.

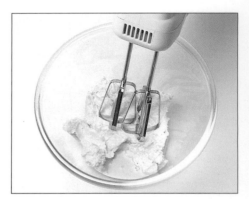

4 ▲ With an electric mixer, cream the butter or margarine and sugar together until light and fluffy. Beat in the eggs, 1 at a time, then the molasses. Stir in the flour mixture, raisins, and walnuts.

5 Spread evenly in the pan. Bake until just set, 15–18 minutes. Let cool in the pan before cutting into bars.

Butterscotch Meringue Bars

MAKES 12

4 tablespoons butter

1 cup dark brown sugar, firmly packed

1 egg

½ teaspoon vanilla extract

½ cup flour

½ teaspoon salt

¼ teaspoon grated nutmeg

FOR THE TOPPING

1 egg white

⅛ teaspoon salt

l tablespoon light corn syrup

½ cup granulated sugar

½ cup walnuts, finely chopped

1 ▲ Combine the butter and brown sugar in a pan and cook until bubbling. Set aside to cool.

2 Preheat oven to 350°F. Line the bottom and sides of an 8-inch square cake pan with wax paper and grease.

3 Beat the egg and vanilla into cooled sugar mixture. Sift over the flour, salt, and nutmeg and fold in. Spread in the bottom of the pan.

4 ▲ For the topping, beat the egg white with the salt until it holds soft peaks. Beat in the corn syrup, then the sugar and continue beating until the mixture holds stiff peaks. Fold in the nuts and spread on top. Bake for 30 minutes. Cut into bars when cool.

Hermits (top), Butterscotch Meringue Bars

MUFFINS & QUICK BREADS

~

Easy to make and satisfying to eat, these muffins and quick breads will fill the house with homey scents and lure your family and friends to linger over breakfast, coffee, or tea — and they are great for snacks or lunch.

Blueberry Muffins

MAKES 12

1¼ cups flour
⅓ cup sugar
2 teaspoons baking powder
¼ teaspoon salt
2 eggs
4 tablespoons butter, melted
¾ cup milk
1 teaspoon vanilla extract
1 teaspoon grated lemon rind
1 cup fresh blueberries

1 Preheat the oven to 400°F.

2 ▼ Grease a 12-cup muffin pan or use paper liners.

3 ▲ Sift the flour, sugar, baking powder, and salt into a bowl.

4 In another bowl, whisk the eggs until blended. Add the melted butter, milk, vanilla, and lemon rind and stir to combine.

5 Make a well in the dry ingredients and pour in the egg mixture. With a large metal spoon, stir just until the flour is moistened, not until smooth.

6 ▲ Fold in the blueberries.

7 ▲ Spoon the batter into the cups, leaving room for the muffins to rise.

8 Bake until the tops spring back when touched lightly, 20–25 minutes. Let cool in the pan for 5 minutes before unmolding.

Apple Cranberry Muffins

MAKES 12

4 tablespoons butter or margarine
1 egg
½ cup sugar
grated rind of 1 large orange
½ cup fresh orange juice
1 cup flour
1 teaspoon baking powder
½ teaspoon baking soda
1 teaspoon ground cinnamon
½ teaspoon grated nutmeg
½ teaspoon ground allspice
¼ teaspoon ground ginger
¼ teaspoon salt
1–2 apples
1 cup cranberries
½ cup walnuts, chopped
confectioners' sugar, for dusting (optional)

1 Preheat the oven to 350°F. Grease a 12-cup muffin pan or use paper liners.

2 Melt the butter or margarine over gentle heat. Set aside to cool.

3 ▲ Place the egg in a mixing bowl and whisk lightly. Add the melted butter or margarine and whisk to combine.

4 Add the sugar, orange rind, and juice. Whisk to blend, then set aside.

5 In a large bowl, sift together the flour, baking powder, baking soda, cinnamon, nutmeg, allspice, ginger, and salt. Set aside.

6 ▲ Quarter, core, and peel the apples. With a sharp knife, chop in a coarse dice to obtain 1¼ cups.

7 Make a well in the dry ingredients and pour in the egg mixture. With a spoon, stir until just blended.

8 ▲ Add the apples, cranberries, and walnuts and stir to blend.

9 Fill the cups three-quarters full and bake until the tops spring back when touched lightly, 25–30 minutes. Transfer to a rack to cool. Dust with confectioners' sugar, if desired.

Chocolate Chip Muffins

MAKES 10

½ cup (1 stick) butter or margarine, at
   room temperature

⅓ cup granulated sugar

2 tablespoons dark brown sugar

2 eggs, at room temperature

1½ cups cake flour

1 teaspoon baking powder

½ cup milk

1 cup semisweet chocolate chips

1 Preheat the oven to 375°F. Grease
10 muffin cups or use paper liners.

2 ▼ With an electric mixer, cream
the butter or margarine until soft. Add
both sugars and beat until light and
fluffy. Beat in the eggs, 1 at a time.

3 Sift together the flour and baking
powder, twice. Fold into the butter
mixture, alternating with the milk.

4 ▲ Divide half the mixture between
the muffin cups. Sprinkle several
chocolate chips on top, then cover
with a spoonful of the batter. To
ensure even baking, half-fill any
empty cups with water.

5 Bake until lightly colored, about 25
minutes. Let stand 5 minutes before
unmolding.

Chocolate Walnut Muffins

MAKES 12

¾ cup (1½ sticks) unsalted butter

4 1-ounce squares semisweet chocolate

1 1-ounce square unsweetened
   chocolate

1 cup granulated sugar

¼ cup dark brown sugar, firmly packed

4 eggs

1 teaspoon vanilla extract

¼ teaspoon almond extract

¾ cup flour

1 cup walnuts, chopped

1 Preheat the oven to 350°F.
Grease a 12-cup muffin pan or
use paper liners.

2 ▼ Melt the butter with the two
chocolates in the top of a double
boiler or in a heatproof bowl set over a
pan of hot water. Transfer to a large
mixing bowl.

3 Stir both the sugars into the
chocolate mixture. Mix in the eggs, 1
at a time, then add the vanilla and
almond extracts.

4 Sift over the flour and fold in.

5 ▲ Stir in the walnuts.

6 Fill the prepared cups almost to the
top and bake until a cake tester
inserted in the center barely comes
out clean, 30–35 minutes. Let stand 5
minutes before transferring to a rack
to cool completely.

Chocolate Chip Muffins (top), Chocolate Walnut Muffins

Raisin Bran Muffins

MAKES 15

4 tablespoons butter or margarine

⅔ cup all-purpose flour

½ cup whole-wheat flour

1½ teaspoons baking soda

⅛ teaspoon salt

1 teaspoon ground cinnamon

½ cup bran

½ cup raisins

⅓ cup dark brown sugar, firmly packed

¼ cup granulated sugar

1 egg

1 cup buttermilk

juice of ½ lemon

1 Preheat the oven to 400°F. Grease 15 muffin cups or use paper liners.

2 ▲ Place the butter or margarine in a saucepan and melt over gentle heat. Set aside.

3 In a mixing bowl, sift together the all-purpose flour, whole-wheat flour, baking soda, salt, and cinnamon.

4 ▲ Add the bran, raisins, and sugars and stir until blended.

5 In another bowl, mix together the egg, buttermilk, lemon juice, and melted butter.

6 ▲ Add the buttermilk mixture to the dry ingredients and stir lightly and quickly just until moistened; do not mix until smooth.

7 ▲ Spoon the batter into the prepared muffin cups, filling them almost to the top. Half-fill any empty cups with water.

8 Bake until golden, 15–20 minutes. Serve warm or at room temperature.

Raspberry Crumble Muffins

MAKES 12

1½ cups flour

¼ cup granulated sugar

¼ cup light brown sugar, firmly packed

2 teaspoons baking powder

⅛ teaspoon salt

1 teaspoon ground cinnamon

½ cup (1 stick) butter, melted

1 egg

½ cup milk

1¼ cups fresh raspberries

grated rind of 1 lemon

FOR THE CRUMBLE TOPPING

¼ cup pecans, finely chopped

¼ cup dark brown sugar, firmly packed

3 tablespoons flour

1 teaspoon ground cinnamon

3 tablespoons butter, melted

1 Preheat the oven to 350°F. Grease a 12-cup muffin pan or use paper liners.

2 Sift the flour into a bowl. Add the sugars, baking powder, salt, and cinnamon and stir to blend.

3 ▲ Make a well in the center. Place the butter, egg, and milk in the well and mix until just combined. Stir in the raspberries and lemon rind. Spoon the batter into the prepared muffin cups, filling them almost to the top.

4 ▼ For the crumble topping, mix the pecans, dark brown sugar, flour, and cinnamon in a bowl. Add the melted butter and stir to blend.

5 ▲ Spoon some of the crumble over each muffin. Bake until browned, about 25 minutes. Transfer to a rack to cool slightly. Serve warm.

Carrot Muffins

MAKES 12

¾ cup margarine, at room temperature

½ cup dark brown sugar, firmly packed

1 egg, at room temperature

1 tablespoon water

2 cups grated carrots

1¼ cups flour

1 teaspoon baking powder

½ teaspoon baking soda

1 teaspoon ground cinnamon

¼ teaspoon grated nutmeg

½ teaspoon salt

1 Preheat the oven to 350°F. Grease a 12-cup muffin pan or use paper liners.

2 With an electric mixer, cream the margarine and sugar until light and fluffy. Beat in the egg and water.

3 ▲ Stir in the carrots.

4 Sift over the flour, baking powder, baking soda, cinnamon, nutmeg, and salt. Stir to blend.

5 ▼ Spoon the batter into the prepared muffin cups, filling them almost to the top. Bake until the tops spring back when touched lightly, about 35 minutes. Let stand 10 minutes before transferring to a rack.

Dried Cherry Muffins

MAKES 16

1 cup plain yogurt

1 cup dried cherries

½ cup (1 stick) butter, at room temperature

¾ cup sugar

2 eggs, at room temperature

1 teaspoon vanilla extract

1¾ cups flour

2 teaspoons baking powder

1 teaspoon baking soda

⅛ teaspoon salt

1 In a mixing bowl, combine the yogurt and cherries. Cover and let stand for 30 minutes.

2 Preheat the oven to 350°F. Grease 16 muffin cups or use paper liners.

3 With an electric mixer, cream the butter and sugar together until light and fluffy.

4 ▼ Add the eggs, 1 at a time, beating well after each addition. Add the vanilla and the cherry mixture and stir to blend. Set aside.

5 ▲ In another bowl, sift together the flour, baking powder, baking soda, and salt. Fold into the cherry mixture in 3 batches; do not overmix.

6 Fill the prepared cups two-thirds full. For even baking, half-fill any empty cups with water. Bake until the tops spring back when touched lightly, about 20 minutes. Transfer to a rack to cool.

Carrot Muffins (top), Dried Cherry Muffins

Oatmeal Buttermilk Muffins

MAKES 12

1 cup rolled oats

1 cup buttermilk

½ cup (1 stick) butter, at room temperature

½ cup dark brown sugar, firmly packed

1 egg, at room temperature

1 cup flour

1 teaspoon baking powder

½ teaspoon baking soda

¼ teaspooon salt

¼ cup raisins

~ **COOK'S TIP** ~

If buttermilk is not available, add 1 teaspoon lemon juice or vinegar per cup of milk. Let the mixture stand a few minutes to curdle.

1 ▲ In a bowl, combine the oats and buttermilk and let soak for 1 hour.

2 ▲ Grease a 12-cup muffin pan or use paper liners.

3 ▲ Preheat the oven to 400°F. With an electric mixer, cream the butter and sugar until light and fluffy. Beat in the egg.

4 In another bowl, sift together the flour, baking powder, baking soda, and salt. Stir into the butter mixture, alternating with the oat mixture. Fold in the raisins. Do not overmix.

5 Fill the prepared cups two-thirds full. Bake until a cake tester inserted in the center comes out clean, 20–25 minutes. Transfer to a rack to cool.

Pumpkin Muffins

MAKES 14

½ cup (1 stick) butter or margarine, at room temperature

¾ cup dark brown sugar, firmly packed

⅓ cup molasses

1 egg, at room temperature, beaten

1 cup cooked or canned pumpkin (about 8 ounces)

1 ¾ cups flour

¼ teaspoon salt

1 teaspoon baking soda

1½ teaspoons ground cinnamon

1 teaspoon grated nutmeg

¼ cup currants or raisins

1 Preheat the oven to 400°F. Grease 14 muffin cups or use paper liners.

2 With an electric mixer, cream the butter or margarine until soft. Add the sugar and molasses and beat until light and fluffy.

3 ▲ Add the egg and pumpkin and stir until well blended.

4 Sift over the flour, salt, baking soda, cinnnamon, and nutmeg. Fold just enough to blend; do not overmix.

5 ▼ Fold in the currants or raisins.

6 Spoon the batter into the prepared muffin cups, filling them three-quarters full.

7 Bake until the tops spring back when touched lightly, 12–15 minutes. Serve warm or cold.

Oatmeal Buttermilk Muffins (top), Pumpkin Muffins

Prune Muffins

MAKES 12

1 egg

1 cup milk

¼ cup vegetable oil

¼ cup granulated sugar

2 tablespoons dark brown sugar

2 cups flour

2 teaspoons baking powder

½ teaspoon salt

¼ teaspoon grated nutmeg

¾ cup cooked pitted prunes, chopped

1 Preheat the oven to 400°F. Grease a 12-cup muffin tin or use paper liners.

2 Break the egg into a mixing bowl and beat with a fork. Beat in the milk and oil.

3 ▼ Stir in the sugars. Set aside.

4 Sift the flour, baking powder, salt, and nutmeg into a mixing bowl. Make a well in the center, pour in the egg mixture and stir until moistened. Do not overmix; the batter should be slightly lumpy.

5 ▲ Fold in the prunes.

6 Fill the prepared cups two-thirds full. Bake until golden brown, about 20 minutes. Let stand 10 minutes before unmolding. Serve warm or at room temperature.

Yogurt Honey Muffins

MAKES 12

4 tablespoons butter

5 tablespoons thin honey

1 cup plain yogurt

1 large egg, at room temperature

grated rind of 1 lemon

¼ cup fresh lemon juice

1 cup all-purpose flour

1 cup whole-wheat flour

1½ teaspoons baking soda

⅛ teaspoon grated nutmeg

~ **VARIATION** ~

For Walnut Yogurt Honey Muffins, add ½ cup chopped walnuts, folded in with the flour. This makes a more substantial muffin.

1 Preheat the oven to 375°F. Grease a 12-cup muffin pan or use paper liners.

2 In a saucepan, melt the butter and honey. Remove from the heat and set aside to cool slightly.

3 ▲ In a bowl, whisk together the yogurt, egg, lemon rind and juice. Add the butter and honey mixture. Set aside.

4 ▲ In another bowl, sift together the dry ingredients.

5 Fold the dry ingredients into the yogurt mixture just to blend.

6 Fill the prepared cups two-thirds full. Bake until the tops spring back when touched lightly, 20–25 minutes. Let cool in the pan for 5 minutes before unmolding. Serve warm or at room temperature.

Prune Muffins (top), Yogurt Honey Muffins

Banana Muffins

MAKES 10

2 cups flour

1 teaspoon baking powder

1 teaspoon baking soda

¼ teaspoon salt

½ teaspoon ground cinnamon

¼ teaspoon grated nutmeg

3 large ripe bananas

1 egg

⅓ cup dark brown sugar, firmly packed

¼ cup vegetable oil

¼ cup raisins

1 Preheat the oven to 375°F.

2 ▼ Line 10 muffin cups with paper liners or grease.

3 Sift together the flour, baking powder, baking soda, salt, nutmeg, and cinnamon. Set aside.

4 ▲ With an electric mixer, beat the peeled bananas at moderate speed until mashed.

5 ▲ Beat in the egg, sugar, and oil.

6 Add the dry ingredients and beat in gradually, on low speed. Mix just until blended. With a wooden spoon, stir in the raisins.

7 Fill the prepared cups two-thirds full. For even baking, half-fill any empty cups with water.

8 ▲ Bake until the tops spring back when touched lightly, 20–25 minutes.

9 Transfer to a rack to cool.

Maple Pecan Muffins

MAKES 20

1¼ cups pecans
2½ cups flour
1 teaspoon baking powder
1 teaspoon baking soda
¼ teaspoon salt
¼ teaspoon ground cinnamon
½ cup granulated sugar
⅓ cup light brown sugar, firmly packed
3 tablespoons maple syrup
⅔ cup (10⅔ tablespoons) butter, at room temperature
3 eggs, at room temperature
1¼ cups buttermilk
60 pecan halves, for decorating

1 Preheat the oven to 350°F. Grease 2 12-cup muffin pans or use paper liners.

2 ▲ Spread the pecans on a baking sheet and toast in the oven for 5 minutes. When cool, chop coarsely and set aside.

~ **VARIATION** ~

For Pecan Spice Muffins, substitute an equal quantity of molasses for the maple syrup. Increase the cinnamon to ½ teaspoon, and add 1 teaspoon ground ginger and ½ teaspoon grated nutmeg, sifted with the flour and other dry ingredients.

3 In a bowl, sift together the flour, baking powder, baking soda, salt, and cinnamon. Set aside.

4 ▲ In a large mixing bowl, combine the granulated sugar, light brown sugar, maple syrup, and butter. Beat with an electric mixer until light and fluffy.

5 Add the eggs, 1 at a time, beating to incorporate thoroughly after each addition.

6 ▲ Pour half the buttermilk and half the dry ingredients into the butter mixture, then stir until blended. Repeat with the remaining buttermilk and dry ingredients.

7 Fold in the chopped pecans.

8 Fill the prepared cups two-thirds full. Top with the pecan halves. For even baking, half-fill any empty cup with water.

9 Bake until puffed up and golden, 20–25 minutes. Let stand 5 minutes before unmolding.

Cheese Muffins

MAKES 9

4 tablespoons butter

1½ cups flour

2 teaspoons baking powder

2 tablespoons sugar

¼ teaspoon salt

1 teaspoon paprika

2 eggs

½ cup milk

1 teaspoon dried thyme

2 ounces sharp cheddar cheese, cut into ½-inch dice

1 Preheat the oven to 375°F. Thickly grease 9 muffin cups or use paper liners.

2 Melt the butter and set aside.

3 ▼ In a mixing bowl, sift together the flour, baking powder, sugar, salt, and paprika.

4 ▲ In another bowl, combine the eggs, milk, melted butter, and thyme, and whisk to blend.

5 Add the milk mixture to the dry ingredients and stir just until moistened; do not mix until smooth.

6 ▲ Place a heaped spoonful of batter into the prepared cups. Drop a few pieces of cheese over each, then top with another spoonful of batter. For even baking, half-fill any empty muffin cups with water.

7 ▲ Bake until puffed and golden, about 25 minutes. Let stand 5 minutes before unmolding onto a rack. Serve warm or at room temperature.

Bacon Cornmeal Muffins

MAKES 14

8 slices bacon

4 tablespoons butter

4 tablespoons margarine

1 cup flour

1 tablespoon baking powder

1 teaspoon sugar

¼ teaspoon salt

1½ cups cornmeal

1 cup milk

2 eggs

1 Preheat the oven to 400°F. Grease 14 muffin cups or use paper liners.

2 ▲ Fry the bacon until crisp. Drain on paper towels, then chop into small pieces. Set aside.

3 Gently melt the butter and margarine and set aside.

4 ▲ Sift the flour, baking powder, sugar, and salt into a large mixing bowl. Stir in the cornmeal, then make a well in the center.

5 In a saucepan, heat the milk to lukewarm. In a small bowl, lightly whisk the eggs, then add to the milk. Stir in the melted fats.

6 ▼ Pour the milk mixture into the center of the well and stir until smooth and well blended.

7 ▲ Fold in the bacon.

8 Spoon the batter into the prepared cups, filling them halfway. Bake until risen and lightly colored, about 20 minutes. Serve hot or warm.

Corn Bread

Makes 1 loaf

1 cup flour

⅓ cup sugar

1 teaspoon salt

1 tablespoon baking powder

1½ cups cornmeal

1½ cups milk

2 eggs

6 tablespoons butter, melted

8 tablespoons margarine, melted

1 Preheat the oven to 400°F. Line the bottom and sides of a 9- × 5-inch loaf pan with wax paper and grease.

2 Sift the flour, sugar, salt, and baking powder into a mixing bowl.

3 ▼ Add the cornmeal and stir to blend. Make a well in the center.

4 ▲ Whisk together the milk, eggs, butter, and margarine. Pour the mixture into the well. Stir until just blended; do not overmix.

5 Pour into the pan and bake until a cake tester inserted in the center comes out clean, about 45 minutes. Serve hot or at room temperature.

Tex-Mex Corn Bread

Makes 9 squares

3–4 whole canned chile peppers, drained

2 eggs

2 cups buttermilk

4 tablespoons butter, melted

½ cup flour

1 teaspoon baking soda

2 teaspoons salt

1½ cups cornmeal

2 cups corn kernels

1 Preheat the oven to 400°F. Line the bottom and sides of a 9-inch square cake pan with wax paper and grease lightly.

2 ▲ With a sharp knife, chop the chiles in a fine dice and set aside.

3 ▲ In a large bowl, whisk the eggs until frothy, then whisk in the buttermilk. Add the melted butter.

4 In another large bowl, sift together the flour, baking soda, and salt. Fold into the buttermilk mixture in 3 batches, then fold in the cornmeal in 3 batches.

5 ▲ Fold in the chiles and corn.

6 Pour the batter into the prepared pan and bake until a cake tester inserted in the middle comes out clean, 25–30 minutes. Let stand for 2–3 minutes before unmolding. Cut into squares and serve warm.

Corn Bread (top), Tex-Mex Corn Bread

Cranberry Orange Bread

MAKES 1 LOAF

2 cups flour

½ cup sugar

1 tablespoon baking powder

½ teaspoon salt

grated rind of 1 large orange

⅔ cup fresh orange juice

2 eggs, lightly beaten

6 tablespoons butter or margarine, melted

1¼ cups fresh cranberries

½ cup walnuts, chopped

1 Preheat the oven to 350°F. Line the bottom and sides of a 9- × 5-inch loaf pan with wax paper and grease.

2 Sift the flour, sugar, baking powder, and salt into a mixing bowl.

3 ▼ Stir in the orange rind.

4 ▲ Make a well in the center and add the orange juice, eggs, and melted butter or margarine. Stir from the center until the ingredients are blended; do not overmix.

5 ▲ Add the cranberries and walnuts and stir until blended.

6 Transfer the batter to the prepared pan and bake until a cake tester inserted in the center comes out clean, 45–50 minutes.

7 ▲ Let cool in the pan for 10 minutes before transferring to a rack to cool completely. Serve thinly sliced, toasted or plain, with butter or cream cheese, and jam.

Date-Nut Bread

MAKES 1 LOAF

1 cup pitted dates, chopped
¾ cup boiling water
4 tablespoons unsalted butter, at room temperature
¼ cup dark brown sugar, firmly packed
¼ cup granulated sugar
1 egg, at room temperature
2 tablespoons brandy
1⅓ cups flour
2 teaspoons baking powder
½ teaspoon salt
¾ teaspoon freshly grated nutmeg
¾ cup pecans, coarsely chopped

1 ▲ Place the dates in a bowl and pour over the boiling water. Set aside to cool.

2 Preheat the oven to 350°F. Line the bottom and sides of a 9- × 5-inch loaf pan with wax paper and grease.

3 ▲ With an electric mixer, cream the butter and sugars until light and fluffy. Beat in the egg and brandy, then set aside.

4 Sift the flour, baking powder, salt, and nutmeg together, 3 times.

5 ▼ Fold the dry ingredients into the sugar mixture in 3 batches, alternating with the dates and water.

6 ▲ Fold in the pecans.

7 Pour the batter into the prepared pan and bake until a cake tester inserted in the center comes out clean, 45–50 minutes. Let cool in the pan for 10 minutes before transferring to a rack to cool completely.

Orange Honey Bread

MAKES 1 LOAF

2½ cups flour

2½ teaspoons baking powder

½ teaspoon baking soda

½ teaspoon salt

2 tablespoons margarine

1 cup thin honey

1 egg, at room temperature, lightly beaten

1½ tablespoons grated orange rind

¾ cup freshly squeezed orange juice

¾ cup walnuts, chopped

1 Preheat the oven to 325°F.

2 Sift together the flour, baking powder, baking soda, and salt.

3 Line the bottom and sides of a 9- × 5-inch loaf pan with wax paper and grease.

4 ▲ With an electric mixer, cream the margarine until soft. Stir in the honey until blended, then stir in the egg. Add the orange rind and stir to combine thoroughly.

5 ▲ Fold the flour mixture into the honey and egg mixture in 3 batches, alternating with the orange juice. Stir in the walnuts.

6 Pour into the pan and bake until a cake tester inserted in the center comes out clean, 60–70 minutes. Let stand 10 minutes before unmolding onto a rack to cool.

Applesauce Bread

MAKES 1 LOAF

1 egg

1 cup applesauce

4 tablespoons butter or margarine, melted

½ cup dark brown sugar, firmly packed

¼ cup granulated sugar

2 cups flour

2 teaspoons baking powder

½ teaspoon baking soda

½ teaspoon salt

1 teaspoon ground cinnamon

½ teaspoon grated nutmeg

½ cup currants or raisins

½ cup pecans, chopped

1 Preheat the oven to 350°F. Line the bottom and sides of a 9- × 5-inch loaf pan with wax paper and grease.

2 ▲ Break the egg into a bowl and beat lightly. Stir in the applesauce, butter or margarine, and both sugars. Set aside.

3 In another bowl, sift together the flour, baking powder, baking soda, salt, cinnamon, and nutmeg. Fold dry ingredients into the applesauce mixture in 3 batches.

4 ▼ Stir in the currants or raisins, and pecans.

5 Pour into the prepared pan and bake until a cake tester inserted in the center comes out clean, about 1 hour. Let stand 10 minutes before unmolding and transferring to a cooling rack.

Orange Honey Bread (top), Applesauce Bread

Lemon Walnut Bread

MAKES 1 LOAF

½ cup (1 stick) butter or margarine, at room temperature

½ cup sugar

2 eggs, at room temperature, separated

grated rind of 2 lemons

2 tablespoons fresh lemon juice

1½ cups cake flour

2 teaspoons baking powder

½ cup milk

½ cup walnuts, chopped

⅛ teaspooon salt

1 Preheat the oven to 350°F. Line the bottom and sides of a 9- × 5-inch loaf pan with wax paper and grease.

2 With an electric mixer, cream the butter or margarine with the sugar until light and fluffy.

3 ▲ Beat in the egg yolks.

4 Add the lemon rind and juice and stir until blended. Set aside.

5 ▲ In another bowl, sift together the flour and baking powder, 3 times. Fold into the butter mixture in 3 batches, alternating with the milk. Fold in the walnuts. Set aside.

6 ▲ Beat the egg whites and salt until stiff peaks form. Fold a large dollop of the egg whites into the walnut mixture to lighten it. Fold in the remaining egg whites carefully just until blended.

7 ▲ Pour the batter into the prepared pan and bake until a cake tester inserted in the center of the loaf comes out clean, 45–50 minutes. Let stand 5 minutes before unmolding onto a rack to cool completely.

Apricot Nut Loaf

MAKES 1 LOAF

¾ cup dried apricots
1 large orange
½ cup raisins
⅔ cup sugar
⅓ cup oil
2 eggs, lightly beaten
2¼ cups flour
2 teaspoons baking powder
½ teaspoon salt
1 teaspoon baking soda
½ cup walnuts, chopped

1 Preheat the oven to 350°F. Line the bottom and sides of a 9- × 5-inch loaf pan with wax paper and grease.

2 Place the apricots in a bowl and add lukewarm water to cover. Let stand for 30 minutes.

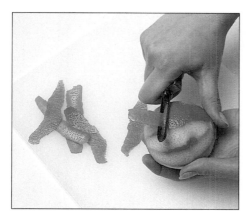

3 ▲ With a vegetable peeler, remove the orange rind, leaving the pith.

4 With a sharp knife, finely chop the orange rind strips.

5 Drain the apricots and chop coarsely. Place in a bowl with the orange rind and raisins. Set aside.

6 Squeeze the peeled orange. Measure the juice and add enough hot water to obtain ¾ cup liquid.

7 ▼ Pour the orange juice mixture over the apricot mixture. Stir in the sugar, oil, and eggs. Set aside.

8 In another bowl, sift together the flour, baking powder, salt, and baking soda. Fold the flour mixture into the apricot mixture in 3 batches.

9 ▲ Stir in the walnuts.

10 Spoon the batter into the prepared pan and bake until a cake tester inserted in the center comes out clean, 55–60 minutes. If the loaf browns too quickly, protect the top with a sheet of foil. Let cool in the pan for 10 minutes before transferring to a rack to cool completely.

Mango Bread

MAKES 2 LOAVES

2 cups flour
2 teaspoons baking soda
2 teaspoons ground cinnamon
½ teaspoon salt
½ cup margarine, at room temperature
3 eggs, at room temperature
1½ cups sugar
½ cup vegetable oil
2 cups chopped ripe mangoes (about 2–3 mangoes)
¾ cup shredded coconut
½ cup raisins

1 Preheat the oven to 350°F. Line the bottom and sides of 2 9- × 5-inch loaf pans with wax paper and grease.

2 Sift together the flour, baking soda, cinnamon, and salt. Set aside.

3 With an electric mixer, cream the margarine until soft.

4 ▼ Beat in the eggs and sugar until light and fluffy. Beat in the oil.

5 Fold the dry ingredients into the creamed ingredients in 3 batches.

6 Fold in the mangoes, ½ cup of the coconut, and the raisins.

7 ▲ Spoon the batter into the pans.

8 Sprinkle over the remaining coconut. Bake until a cake tester inserted in the center comes out clean, 50–60 minutes. Let stand for 10 minutes before transferring to a rack to cool completely.

Zucchini Bread

MAKES 1 LOAF

4 tablespoons butter
3 eggs
1 cup corn oil
1½ cups sugar
2 cups grated unpeeled zucchini
2 cups flour
2 teaspoons baking soda
1 teaspoon baking powder
1 teaspoon salt
1 teaspoon ground cinnamon
1 teaspoon grated nutmeg
¼ teaspoon ground cloves
1 cup walnuts, chopped

1 Preheat the oven to 350°F. Line the bottom and sides of a 9- × 5-inch loaf pan with wax paper and grease.

2 ▲ In a saucepan, melt the butter over low heat. Set aside.

3 With an electric mixer, beat the eggs and oil together until thick. Beat in the sugar. Stir in the melted butter and zucchini. Set aside.

4 ▲ In another bowl, sift all the dry ingredients together 3 times. Carefully fold into the zucchini mixture. Fold in the walnuts.

5 Pour into the pan and bake until a cake tester inserted in the center comes out clean, 60–70 minutes. Let stand 10 minutes before unmolding.

Mango Bread (top), Zucchini Bread

Whole-Wheat Banana Nut Bread

MAKES 1 LOAF

½ cup (1 stick) butter, at room temperature

½ cup granulated sugar

2 eggs, at room temperature

1 cup all-purpose flour

1 teaspoon baking soda

¼ teaspoon salt

1 teaspoon ground cinnamon

½ cup whole-wheat flour

3 large ripe bananas

1 teaspoon vanilla extract

½ cup pecans, chopped

1 Preheat the oven to 350°F. Line the bottom and sides of a 9- × 5-inch loaf pan with wax paper and grease.

2 With an electric mixer, cream the butter and sugar together until light and fluffy.

3 ▲ Add the eggs, 1 at a time, beating well after each addition.

4 Sift the all-purpose flour, baking soda, salt, and cinnamon over the butter mixture and stir to blend.

5 ▲ Stir in the whole-wheat flour.

6 ▲ With a fork, mash the bananas to a purée, then stir into the batter. Stir in the vanilla and pecans.

7 ▲ Pour the batter into the prepared pan and spread level.

8 Bake until a cake tester inserted in the center comes out clean, 50–60 minutes. Let stand 10 minutes before transferring to a rack.

Dried Fruit Loaf

MAKES 1 LOAF

2½ cups mixed dried fruit, such as currants, raisins, chopped dried apricots, and dried cherries

1¼ cups cold strong tea

1 cup dark brown sugar, firmly packed

grated rind and juice of 1 small orange

grated rind and juice of 1 lemon

1 egg, lightly beaten

1¾ cups flour

1 tablespoon baking powder

⅛ teaspoon salt

1 ▲ In a bowl, toss together all the dried fruit, pour over the tea, and leave to soak overnight.

2 Preheat the oven to 350°F. Line the bottom and sides of a 9- × 5-inch loaf pan with wax paper and grease.

3 ▲ Strain the fruit, reserving the liquid. In a bowl, combine the sugar, orange and lemon rind, and fruit.

4 ▼ Pour the orange and lemon juice into a measuring cup; if the quantity is less than 1 cup, complete with the soaking liquid.

5 Stir the citrus juices and egg into the dried fruit mixture.

6 In another bowl, sift together the flour, baking powder, and salt. Stir into the fruit mixture until blended.

7 Transfer to the prepared pan and bake until a cake tester inserted in the center comes out clean, about 1¼ hours. Let stand 10 minutes before unmolding.

Blueberry Streusel Bread

MAKES 8 PIECES

4 tablespoons butter or margarine, at room temperature

¾ cup sugar

1 egg, at room temperature

½ cup milk

2 cups flour

2 teaspoons baking powder

½ teaspoon salt

2 cups fresh blueberries

FOR THE TOPPING

½ cup sugar

⅓ cup flour

½ teaspoon ground cinnamon

4 tablespoons butter, cut in pieces

1 Preheat the oven to 375°F. Grease a 9-inch square baking dish.

2 With an electric mixer, cream the butter or margarine with the sugar until light and fluffy. Add the egg, beat to combine, then mix in the milk until blended.

3 ▼ Sift over the flour, baking powder, and salt and stir just enough to blend the ingredients.

4 ▲ Add the blueberries and stir.

5 Transfer to the baking dish.

6 ▲ For the topping, place the sugar, flour, cinnamon, and butter in a mixing bowl. Cut in with a pastry blender until the mixture resembles coarse crumbs.

7 ▲ Sprinkle the topping over the batter in the pan.

8 Bake until a cake tester inserted in the center comes out clean, about 45 minutes. Serve warm or cold.

Chocolate Chip Walnut Loaf

MAKES 1 LOAF

½ cup granulated sugar

¾ cup cake flour

1 teaspoon baking powder

4 tablespoons potato flour or cornstarch

9 tablespoons butter, at room temperature

2 eggs, at room temperature

1 teaspoon vanilla extract

2 tablespoons currants or raisins

¼ cup walnuts, finely chopped

grated rind of ½ lemon

¼ cup semisweet chocolate chips

confectioners' sugar, for dusting

1 Preheat the oven to 350°F. Line an 8½- × 4½-inch loaf pan with wax paper and grease.

2 ▲ Sprinkle 1½ tablespoons of the granulated sugar into the pan and tilt to distribute the sugar in an even layer over the bottom and sides. Shake out any excess.

~ **COOK'S TIP** ~

For best results, the eggs should be at room temperature. If they are too cold when folded into the creamed butter mixture, it may separate. If this happens, add a spoonful of the flour to help stabilize the mixture.

3 ▼ Sift together the cake flour, baking powder, and potato flour or cornstarch, 3 times. Set aside.

4 With an electric mixer, cream the butter until soft. Add the remaining sugar and continue beating until light and fluffy. Add the eggs, 1 at a time, beating to incorporate thoroughly after each addition.

5 Gently fold the dry ingredients into the butter mixture, in 3 batches; do not overmix.

6 ▲ Fold in the vanilla, currants or raisins, walnuts, lemon rind, and chocolate chips until just blended.

7 Pour the batter into the prepared pan and bake until a cake tester inserted in the center comes out clean, 45–50 minutes. Let cool in the pan for 5 minutes before transferring to a rack to cool completely. Dust over an even layer of confectioners' sugar before serving.

Glazed Banana Spice Loaf

MAKES 1 LOAF

1 large ripe banana

½ cup (1 stick) butter, at room
temperature

¾ cup granulated sugar

2 eggs, at room temperature

1½ cups flour

1 teaspoon salt

1 teaspoon baking soda

½ teaspoon grated nutmeg

¼ teaspoon ground allspice

¼ teaspoon ground cloves

¾ cup sour cream

1 teaspoon vanilla extract

FOR THE GLAZE

1 cup confectioners' sugar

1–2 tablespoons fresh lemon juice

1 Preheat the oven to 350°F. Line an 8½- × 4½-inch loaf pan with wax paper and grease.

2 ▼ With a fork, mash the banana in a bowl. Set aside.

3 With an electric mixer, cream the butter and sugar until light and fluffy. Add the eggs, 1 at a time, beating to blend well after each addition.

4 Sift together the flour, salt, baking soda, nutmeg, allspice, and cloves. Add to the butter mixture and stir to combine well.

5 ▲ Add the sour cream, banana, and vanilla and mix just enough to blend. Pour into the prepared pan.

6 ▲ Bake until the top springs back when touched lightly, 45–50 minutes. Let cool in the pan for 10 minutes before unmolding.

7 ▲ For the glaze, combine the confectioners' sugar and lemon juice, then stir until smooth.

8 To glaze, place the cooled loaf on a rack set over a baking sheet. Pour the glaze over the top of the bread and allow to set.

Sweet Sesame Loaf

MAKES 1 OR 2 LOAVES

⅔ cup sesame seeds

2 cups flour

2½ teaspoons baking powder

1 teaspoon salt

4 tablespoons butter or margarine, at
 room temperature

⅔ cup sugar

2 eggs, at room temperature

grated rind of 1 lemon

1½ cups milk

1 Preheat the oven to 350°F. Line a
10- × 6-inch baking pan, or 2 small
loaf pans, with wax paper and grease.

2 ▲ Reserve 2 tablespoons of the
sesame seeds. Spread the rest on a
baking sheet and bake until lightly
toasted, about 10 minutes.

3 Sift the flour, salt, and baking
powder into a bowl.

4 ▲ Stir in the toasted sesame seeds
and set aside.

5 With an electric mixer, cream the
butter or margarine and sugar together
until light and fluffy. Beat in the eggs,
then stir in the lemon rind and milk.

6 ▼ Pour the milk mixture over the
dry ingredients and fold in with a large
metal spoon until just blended.

7 ▲ Pour into the pan and sprinkle
over the reserved sesame seeds.

8 Bake until a cake tester inserted in
the center comes out clean, about 1
hour. Let cool in the pan for 10
minutes before unmolding.

Whole-Wheat Scones

MAKES 16

¾ cup (1½ sticks) cold butter

2 cups whole-wheat flour

1 cup all-purpose flour

2 tablespoons sugar

½ teaspoon salt

2½ teaspoons baking soda

2 eggs

¾ cup buttermilk

¼ cup raisins

1 Preheat the oven to 400°F. Grease and flour a large baking sheet.

2 ▲ Cut the butter into small pieces.

3 Combine the dry ingredients in a bowl. Add the butter and cut in with a pastry blender until the mixture resembles coarse crumbs. Set aside.

4 In another bowl, whisk together the eggs and buttermilk. Set aside 2 tablespoons for glazing.

5 Stir the remaining egg mixture into the dry ingredients until it just holds together. Stir in the raisins.

6 Roll out the dough about ¾ inch thick. Stamp out circles with a cookie cutter. Place on the prepared sheet and brush with the glaze.

7 Bake until golden, 12–15 minutes. Allow to cool slightly before serving. Split in two with a fork while still warm and spread with butter and jam, if wished.

Orange Raisin Scones

MAKES 16

2 cups flour

1½ tablespoons baking powder

⅓ cup sugar

½ teaspoon salt

5 tablespoons butter, diced

5 tablespoons margarine, diced

grated rind of 1 large orange

⅓ cup raisins

½ cup buttermilk

milk, for glazing

1 Preheat the oven to 425°F. Grease and flour a large baking sheet

2 Combine the dry ingredients in a large bowl. Add the butter and margarine and cut in with a pastry blender until the mixture resembles coarse crumbs.

3 ▲ Add the orange rind and raisins.

4 Gradually stir in the buttermilk to form a soft dough.

5 ▲ Roll out the dough about ¾ inch thick. Stamp out circles with a cookie cutter.

6 ▲ Place on the prepared sheet and brush the tops with milk.

7 Bake until golden, 12–15 minutes. Serve hot or warm, with butter or whipped cream, and jam.

> **~ COOK'S TIP ~**
>
> For light tender scones, handle the dough as little as possible. If you wish, split the scones when cool and toast them under a preheated broiler. Butter them while still hot.

Whole-Wheat Scones (top), Orange Raisin Scones

Buttermilk Biscuits

Makes 15

1½ cups flour

1 teaspoon salt

1 teaspoon baking powder

½ teaspoon baking soda

4 tablespoons cold butter or margarine

¾ cup buttermilk

1 Preheat the oven to 425°F. Grease a baking sheet.

2 Sift the dry ingredients into a bowl. Cut in the butter or margarine with a pastry blender until the mixture resembles coarse crumbs.

3 ▼ Gradually pour in the buttermilk, stirring with a fork to form a soft dough.

4 ▲ Roll out about ½ inch thick.

5 Stamp out 2-inch circles with a cookie cutter.

6 Place on the prepared tray and bake until golden, 12–15 minutes. Serve warm or at room temperature.

Baking Powder Biscuits

Makes 8

1⅓ cups flour

2 tablespoons sugar

3 teaspoons baking powder

⅛ teaspoon salt

5 tablespoons cold butter, cut in pieces

½ cup milk

1 Preheat the oven to 425°F. Grease a baking sheet.

2 ▲ Sift the flour, sugar, baking powder, and salt into a bowl.

3 Cut in the butter with a pastry blender until the mixture resembles coarse crumbs.

4 Pour in the milk and stir with a fork to form a soft dough.

~ **VARIATION** ~

For Berry Shortcake, split the biscuits in half while still warm. Butter one half, top with lightly sugared fresh berries, such as strawberries, raspberries or blueberries, and sandwich with the other half. Serve with dollops of whipped cream.

5 ▲ Roll out the dough about ¼ inch thick. Stamp out circles with a 2½-inch cookie cutter.

6 Place on the prepared sheet and bake until golden, about 12 minutes. Serve hot or warm, with butter for meals; to accompany tea or coffee, serve with butter and jam.

Buttermilk Biscuits (top), Baking Powder Biscuits

Herb Popovers

MAKES 12

3 eggs

1 cup milk

2 tablespoons butter, melted

¾ cup flour

⅛ teaspoon salt

1 small sprig each mixed fresh herbs, such as chives, tarragon, dill, and parsley

1 Preheat the oven to 425°F. Grease 12 small ramekins or popover cups.

2 With an electric mixer, beat the eggs until blended. Beat in the milk and melted butter.

3 Sift together the flour and salt, then beat into the egg mixture to combine thoroughly.

4 ▼ Strip the herb leaves from the stems and chop finely. Mix together and measure out 2 tablespoons. Stir the herbs into the batter.

5 ▲ Fill the prepared cups half-full.

6 Bake until golden, 25–30 minutes. Do not open the oven door during baking time or the popovers may fall. For drier popovers, pierce each one with a knife after the 30 minute baking time and bake for 5 minutes more. Serve hot.

Cheese Popovers

MAKES 12

3 eggs

1 cup milk

2 tablespoons butter, melted

¾ cup flour

¼ teaspoon salt

¼ teaspoon paprika

6 tablespoons freshly grated Parmesan cheese

1 Preheat the oven to 425°F. Grease 12 small ramekins or popover cups.

2 ▲ With an electric mixer, beat the eggs until blended. Beat in the milk and melted butter.

3 ▲ Sift together the flour, salt, and paprika, then beat into the egg mixture. Add the cheese and stir.

4 Fill the prepared cups half-full and bake until golden, 25–30 minutes. Do not open the oven door during baking or the popovers may fall. For drier popovers, pierce each one with a knife after the 30 minute baking time and bake for 5 minutes more. Serve hot.

~ VARIATION ~

To make Yorkshire Pudding Popovers, as an accompaniment for roast beef, omit the cheese, and use 4–6 tablespoons of the pan drippings to replace the butter. Put them into the oven in time to serve warm with the beef.

Herb Popovers (top), Cheese Popovers

Yeast Breads

~

*Though the pace of today's life may leave less time for baking,
breadmaking can be the best antidote. The process is simple
yet infinitely variable, as the loaves that follow prove.
Roll up your sleeves and create a tradition.*

White Bread

MAKES 2 LOAVES

¼ cup lukewarm water

1 package active dry yeast

2 tablespoons sugar

2 cups lukewarm milk

2 tablespoons butter or margarine, at room temperature

2 teaspoons salt

6–6½ cups flour

1 Combine the water, yeast, and 1 tablespoon of sugar in a measuring cup and let stand 15 minutes until the mixture is frothy.

2 ▼ Pour the milk into a large bowl. Add the remaining sugar, the butter or margarine, and salt. Stir in the yeast mixture.

3 Stir in the flour, 1 cup at a time, until a stiff dough is obtained. Alternatively, use a food processor.

4 ▲ Transfer the dough to a floured surface. To knead, push the dough away from you with the palm of your hand, then fold it toward you, and push it away again. Repeat until the dough is smooth and elastic.

5 Place the dough in a large greased bowl, cover with a plastic bag, and leave to rise in a warm place until doubled in volume, 2–3 hours.

6 Grease 2 9- × 5-inch loaf pans.

7 ▲ Punch down the risen dough with your fist and divide in half. Form into loaf shapes and place in the pans, seam-side down. Cover and let rise in a warm place until almost doubled in volume, about 45 minutes.

8 Preheat the oven to 375°F.

9 Bake until firm and brown, 45–50 minutes. Unmold and tap the bottom of a loaf: if it sounds hollow the loaf is done. If necessary, return to the oven and bake a few minutes more.

10 Let cool on a rack.

Country Bread

MAKES 2 LOAVES

2½ cups whole-wheat flour	
2½ cups all-purpose flour	
1 cup strong flour	
4 teaspoons salt	
4 tablespoons butter, at room temperature	
2 cups lukewarm milk	

FOR THE STARTER

1 package active dry yeast	
1 cup lukewarm water	
1 cup all-purpose flour	
¼ teaspoon sugar	

1 ▲ For the starter, combine the yeast, water, flour, and sugar in a bowl and stir with a fork. Cover and leave in a warm place for 2–3 hours, or leave overnight in a cool place.

2 Place the flours, salt, and butter in a food processor and process just until blended, 1–2 minutes.

3 Stir together the milk and starter, then slowly pour into the processor, with the motor running, until the mixture forms a dough. If necessary, add more water. Alternatively, the dough can be mixed by hand. Transfer to a floured surface and knead until smooth and elastic.

4 Place in an ungreased bowl, cover with a plastic bag, and leave to rise in a warm place until doubled in volume, about 1½ hours.

5 Transfer to a floured surface and knead briefly. Return to the bowl and leave to rise until tripled in volume, about 1½ hours.

6 ▲ Divide the dough in half. Cut off one-third of the dough from each half and shape into balls. Shape the larger remaining portion of each half into balls. Grease a baking sheet.

7 ▲ For each loaf, top the large ball with the small ball and press the center with the handle of a wooden spoon to secure. Cover with a plastic bag, slash the top, and leave to rise.

8 Preheat the oven to 400°F. Dust the dough with whole-wheat flour and bake until the top is browned and the bottom sounds hollow when tapped, 45–50 minutes. Cool on a rack.

Braided Loaf

MAKES 1 LOAF

1 package active dry yeast
1 teaspoon honey
1 cup lukewarm milk
4 tablespoons butter, melted
3 cups flour
1 teaspoon salt
1 egg, lightly beaten
1 egg yolk beaten with 1 teaspoon milk, for glazing

1 ▼ Combine the yeast, honey, milk, and butter, stir, and leave for 15 minutes to dissolve.

2 In a large bowl, mix together the flour and salt. Make a well in the center and add the yeast mixture and egg. With a wooden spoon, stir from the center, incorporating flour with each turn, to obtain a rough dough.

3 Transfer to a floured surface and knead until smooth and elastic. Place in a clean bowl, cover, and leave to rise in a warm place until doubled in volume, about 1½ hours.

4 Grease a baking sheet. Punch down the dough and divide into three equal pieces. Roll to shape each piece into a long thin strip.

5 ▲ Begin braiding from the center strip, tucking in the ends. Cover loosely and leave to rise in a warm place for 30 minutes.

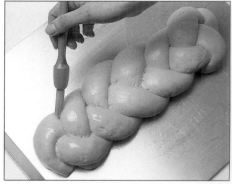

6 ▲ Preheat the oven to 375°F. Place the bread in a cool place while oven heats. Brush with the glaze and bake until golden, 40–45 minutes. Set on a rack to cool completely.

Sesame Seed Bread

MAKES 1 LOAF

2 teaspoons active dry yeast

1¼ cups lukewarm water

1½ cups all-purpose flour

1½ cups whole-wheat flour

2 teaspoons salt

½ cup toasted sesame seeds

milk, for glazing

2 tablespoons sesame seeds, for
   sprinkling

1 Combine the the yeast and ¼ cup
of the water and leave to dissolve. Mix
the flours and salt in a large bowl.
Make a well in the center and pour in
the yeast and the remaining water.

2 ▲ With a wooden spoon, stir from
the center, incorporating flour with
each turn, to obtain a rough dough.

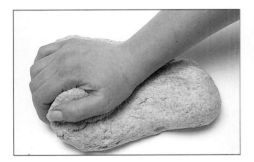

3 ▲ Transfer to a floured surface. To
knead, push the dough away from you
with the palm of your hand, then fold
it towards you, and push away again.
Repeat until smooth and elastic, then
return to the bowl and cover with a
plastic bag. Leave in a warm place
until doubled in volume, 1½–2 hours.

4 ▲ Grease a 9-inch cake pan.
Punch down the dough and knead in
the sesame seeds. Divide the dough
into 16 balls and place in the pan.
Cover with a plastic bag and leave in a
warm place until risen above the rim
of the pan.

5 ▼ Preheat the oven to 425°F.
Brush the top of the loaf with milk
and sprinkle with the sesame seeds.
Bake for 15 minutes. Lower the heat
to 375°F and bake until the bottom
sounds hollow when tapped, about
30 minutes more. Cool on a rack.

Whole-Wheat Bread

MAKES 1 LOAF

4½ cups whole-wheat flour

2 teaspoons salt

4 teaspoons active dry yeast

1¾ cups lukewarm water

2 tablespoons honey

3 tablespoons oil

½ cup wheat germ

milk, for glazing

1 Combine the flour and salt in a bowl and place in a low oven (about 150°F) until warmed, 8–10 minutes.

2 Meanwhile, combine the yeast with ¾ cup of the water in a small bowl and leave to dissolve.

3 ▼ Make a well in the center of the flour. Pour in the yeast mixture, the remaining water, honey, oil, and wheat germ. With a wooden spoon, stir from the center until smooth.

4 Transfer the dough to a lightly floured surface and knead just enough to shape into a loaf.

5 ▲ Grease a 9- × 5-inch loaf pan, place the dough in the pan, and cover with a plastic bag. Leave to rise in a warm place until dough is about 1 inch above rim of pan, about 1 hour.

6 Preheat the oven to 400°F. Bake until the top is browned and the bottom sounds hollow when tapped, 35–40 minutes. Cool on a rack.

Rye Bread

MAKES 1 LOAF

2 cups rye flour

2 cups boiling water

½ cup molasses

5 tablespoons butter, cut in pieces

1 tablespoon salt

2 tablespoons caraway seeds

1 package active dry yeast

½ cup lukewarm water

6–6¼ cups all-purpose flour

cornmeal, for dusting

~ COOK'S TIP ~

To bring out the flavor of the caraway seeds, toast them lightly. Spread the seeds on a baking tray and place in a preheated 325°F oven for about 7 minutes.

1 ▲ Mix the rye flour, boiling water, molasses, butter, salt and caraway seeds in a large bowl. Leave to cool.

2 In another bowl, mix the yeast and lukewarm water and leave to dissolve. Stir into the rye flour mixture. Stir in just enough all-purpose flour to obtain a stiff dough. If it becomes too stiff, stir with your hands.

3 Transfer to a floured surface and knead until the dough is no longer sticky and is smooth and shiny.

4 Place in a greased bowl, cover with a plastic bag, and leave in a warm place until doubled in volume. Punch down the dough, cover, and let rise again for 30 minutes.

5 Preheat the oven to 350°F. Dust a baking sheet with cornmeal.

6 ▼ Shape the dough into a ball. Place on the sheet and score several times across the top. Bake until the bottom sounds hollow when tapped, about 40 minutes. Cool on a rack.

Whole-Wheat Bread (top), Rye Bread

Buttermilk Graham Bread

MAKES 2 LOAVES

1 package active dry yeast

½ cup lukewarm water

2 cups graham flour

3 cups all-purpose flour

1 cup cornmeal

2 teaspoons salt

2 tablespoons sugar

4 tablespoons butter, at room temperature

2 cups lukewarm buttermilk

1 beaten egg, for glazing

sesame seeds, for sprinkling

1 Combine the yeast and water, stir, and leave for 15 minutes to dissolve.

2 ▲ Mix the graham flour, all-purpose flour, cornmeal, salt, and sugar in a large bowl. Make a well in the center and pour in the yeast mixture, the butter and buttermilk.

3 ▲ Stir from the center, mixing in the flour until a rough dough is formed. If too stiff, use your hands.

4 ▲ Transfer to a floured surface and knead until smooth. Place in a clean bowl, cover, and leave in a warm place until doubled, 2–3 hours.

5 ▲ Grease 2 8-inch square baking pans. Punch down the dough. Divide into 8 equal pieces and roll the pieces into balls. Place 4 balls in each pan. Cover and leave in a warm place until the dough rises above the rim of the pans, about 1 hour.

6 Preheat the oven to 375°F. Brush with the glaze, then sprinkle over the sesame seeds. Bake until the bottoms sound hollow when tapped, about 50 minutes. Cool on a rack.

Multi-Grain Bread

MAKES 2 LOAVES

1 package active dry yeast

¼ cup lukewarm water

1 cup rolled oats

2 cups milk

2 teaspoons salt

¼ cup oil

¼ cup brown sugar, firmly packed

2 tablespoons honey

2 eggs, lightly beaten

½ cup wheat germ

1 cup soy flour

2 cups whole-wheat flour

3–3½ cups all-purpose flour

1 Combine the yeast and water, stir, and leave for 15 minutes to dissolve.

2 ▲ Place the oats in a large bowl. Heat the milk until scalded, then pour over the oats.

3 Stir in the salt, oil, sugar, and honey. Cool the mixture to 85°F.

~ **VARIATION** ~

Different flours may be used in this recipe, such as rye, barley, buckwheat or cornmeal. Try replacing the wheat germ and the soy flour with one or two of these, using the same total amount.

4 ▲ Stir in the yeast mixture, eggs, wheat germ, soy, and whole-wheat flours. Gradually stir in enough all-purpose flour to obtain a rough dough.

5 Transfer the dough to a floured surface and knead, adding flour if necessary, until smooth and elastic. Return to a clean bowl, cover, and leave to rise in a warm place until doubled in volume, about 2½ hours.

6 Grease 2 8½- × 4½-inch bread pans. Punch down the risen dough with your fist and knead briefly.

7 Divide the dough into quarters. Roll each quarter into a cylinder 1½ inch thick. Twist together 2 cylinders and place in a pan; repeat for remaining cylinders.

8 Cover and leave to rise until doubled in size, about 1 hour.

9 Preheat the oven to 375°F.

10 ▲ Bake until the bottoms sound hollow when tapped lightly, 45–50 minutes. Cool on a rack.

Potato Bread

MAKES 2 LOAVES

4 teaspoons active dry yeast

1 cup lukewarm milk

½ pound potatoes, boiled (reserve 1 cup of potato cooking liquid)

2 tablespoons oil

4 teaspoons salt

6–6½ cups flour

1 Combine the yeast and milk in a large bowl and leave to dissolve, about 15 minutes.

2 Meanwhile, mash the potatoes.

3 ▲ Add the potatoes, oil, and salt to the yeast mixture and mix well. Stir in 1 cup of the cooking water, then stir in the flour, 1 cup at a time, to form a stiff dough.

4 Transfer to a floured surface and knead until smooth and elastic. Return to the bowl, cover, and leave in a warm place until doubled in size, 1–1½ hours. Punch down, then leave to rise for another 40 minutes.

5 Grease 2 9- × 5-inch loaf pans. Roll the dough into 20 small balls. Place two rows of balls in each pan. Leave until the dough has risen above the rim of the pans.

6 Preheat the oven to 400°F. Bake for 10 minutes, then lower the heat to 375°F and bake until the bottoms sound hollow when tapped, about 40 minutes. Cool on a rack.

Irish Soda Bread

MAKES 1 LOAF

2 cups all-purpose flour

1 cup whole-wheat flour

1 teaspoon baking soda

1 teaspoon salt

2 tablespoons butter or margarine, at room temperature

1¼ cups buttermilk

1 tablespoon all-purpose flour, for dusting

1 Preheat the oven to 400°F. Grease a baking sheet.

2 Sift the flours, baking soda, and salt together into a bowl. Make a well in the center and add the butter or margarine and buttermilk. Working outward from the center, stir with a fork until a soft dough is formed.

3 ▲ With floured hands, gather the dough into a ball.

4 ▲ Transfer to a floured surface and knead for 3 minutes. Shape the dough into a large round.

5 ▲ Place on the baking sheet. Cut a cross in the top with a sharp knife.

6 ▲ Dust with flour. Bake until brown, 40–50 minutes. Transfer to a rack to cool.

Potato Bread (top), Irish Soda Bread

Anadama Bread

MAKES 2 LOAVES

1 package active dry yeast

4 tablespoons lukewarm water

½ cup cornmeal

3 tablespoons butter or margarine

4 tablespoons molasses

¾ cup boiling water

1 egg

3 cups flour

2 teaspoons salt

1 Combine the yeast and lukewarm water, stir well, and leave for 15 minutes to dissolve.

2 ▼ Meanwhile, combine the cornmeal, butter or margarine, molasses, and boiling water in a large bowl. Add the yeast, egg, and half of the flour. Stir together to blend.

3 ▲ Stir in the remaining flour and salt. When the dough becomes too stiff, stir with your hands until it comes away from the sides of the bowl. If it is too sticky, add more flour; if too stiff, add a little water.

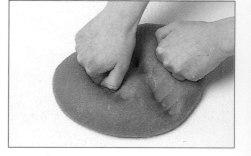

4 ▲ Knead until smooth and elastic. Place in a bowl, cover with a plastic bag, and leave in a warm place until doubled in volume, 2–3 hours.

5 Grease 2 7- × 3-inch bread pans. Punch down the dough with your fist. Shape into 2 loaves and place in the pans, seam-side down. Cover and leave in a warm place until risen above the top of the pans, 1–2 hours.

6 ▲ Preheat the oven to 375°F. Bake for 50 minutes. Unmold and cool on a rack, or set across the pan to cool.

Oatmeal Bread

MAKES 2 LOAVES

2 cups milk
2 tablespoons butter
¼ cup dark brown sugar, firmly packed
2 teaspoons salt
1 package active dry yeast
¼ cup lukewarm water
2½ cups rolled oats (not quick-cooking)
5–6 cups flour

1 ▲ Scald the milk. Remove from the heat and stir in the butter, brown sugar and salt. Leave until lukewarm.

2 Combine the yeast and warm water in a large bowl and leave until the yeast is dissolved and the mixture is frothy. Stir in the milk mixture.

3 ▲ Add 2 cups of the oats and enough flour to obtain a soft dough.

4 Transfer to a floured surface and knead until smooth and elastic.

5 ▲ Place in a greased bowl, cover with a plastic bag, and leave until doubled in volume, 2–3 hours.

6 Grease a large baking sheet. Transfer the dough to a lightly floured surface and divide in half.

7 ▼ Shape into rounds. Place on the baking sheet, cover with a dish towel, and leave to rise until doubled in volume, about 1 hour.

8 Preheat the oven to 400°F. Score the tops and sprinkle with the remaining oats. Bake until the bottoms sound hollow when tapped, 45–50 minutes. Cool on racks.

Sourdough Bread

MAKES 1 LOAF

3 cups flour
1 tablespoon salt
½ cup lukewarm water
1 cup Sourdough Starter (see below)

1 ▲ Combine the flour and salt in a large bowl. Make a well in the center and add the starter and water. With a wooden spoon, stir from the center, incorporating more flour with each turn, to obtain a rough dough.

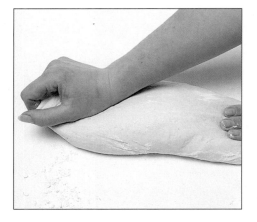

2 ▲ Transfer the dough to a floured surface. To knead, push the dough away from you with the palm of your hand, then fold it towards you, and push it away again. Repeat the process until the dough has become smooth and elastic.

3 Place in a clean bowl, cover, and leave to rise in a warm place until doubled in volume, about 2 hours.

4 Lightly grease an 8½- × 4½-inch bread pan.

5 ▼ Punch down the dough with your fist. Knead briefly, then form into a loaf shape and place in the pan, seam-side down. Cover with a plastic bag, and leave to rise in a warm place until the dough rises above the rim of the pan, about 1½ hours.

6 Preheat the oven to 425°F. Dust the top of the loaf with flour, then score lengthwise. Bake for 15 minutes. Lower the heat to 375°F and bake until the bottom sounds hollow when tapped, about 30 minutes more.

Sourdough Starter

MAKES 3 CUPS

1 package active dry yeast
2½ cups lukewarm water
1½ cups flour

~ COOK'S TIP ~

After using, or after 3 days at room temperature, feed the starter with a handful of flour and enough water to restore it to a thick batter. The starter can be refrigerated for up to 1 week, but must be brought back to room temperature before using.

1 ▲ For the starter, combine the yeast and water, stir, and leave for 15 minutes to dissolve.

2 ▼ Sprinkle over the flour and whisk until it forms a batter; it does not have to be smooth. Cover and leave to rise in a warm place for at least 24 hours, or preferably 2–4 days, before using.

Sourdough French Loaves

MAKES 2 LOAVES

2 teaspoons active dry yeast
1½ cups lukewarm water
1 cup Sourdough Starter (see page 112)
6 cups flour
1 tablespoon salt
1 teaspoon sugar
cornmeal, for sprinkling
1 teaspoon cornstarch
½ cup water

1 In a large bowl, combine the yeast and lukewarm water, stir, and leave for 15 minutes to dissolve.

2 ▲ Pour in the sourdough starter. Add 4 cups of the flour, salt, and sugar and stir until smooth. Cover the bowl with a plastic bag and leave to rise in a warm place until doubled in volume, about 1½ hours.

3 Stir in just enough flour to obtain a rough dough. Transfer to a floured surface and knead until the dough is smooth and elastic. Divide in half, then shape each half into a 14-inch cylinder with rounded ends.

4 ▲ Place loaves on a wooden board or tray sprinkled with cornmeal. Cover loosely with a dish towel or wax paper and leave to rise in a warm place until nearly doubled in volume.

5 Preheat the oven to 425°F.

6 Place a 15- × 12-inch baking sheet in the oven and a shallow baking dish on the bottom of the oven half-filled with hot water.

7 In a small saucepan, bring the cornstarch and water to a boil, stirring constantly. Set aside.

8 ▲ With a sharp knife, make several diagonal slashes across the loaves. Slide onto the hot baking sheet and brush over the cornstarch mixture. Bake until the tops are golden and the bottoms sound hollow when tapped, about 25 minutes. Cool on a rack.

Sourdough Rye Bread

MAKES 2 LOAVES

2 teaspoons active dry yeast

½ cup lukewarm water

2 tablespoons butter, melted

1 tablespoon salt

1 cup whole-wheat flour

3½–4 cups all-purpose flour

1 egg mixed with 1 tablespoon of water, for glazing

FOR THE STARTER

1 package active dry yeast

1½ cups lukewarm water

3 tablespoons molasses

2 tablespoons caraway seeds

2½ cups rye flour

1 For the starter, combine the yeast and water, stir, and leave for 15 minutes to dissolve.

2 ▲ Stir in the molasses, caraway seeds, and rye flour. Cover and leave in a warm place for 2–3 days.

3 In a large bowl, combine the yeast and water, stir, and leave for 10 minutes. Stir in the melted butter, salt, whole-wheat flour, and 3½ cups of the all-purpose flour.

4 ▲ Make a well in the center and pour in the starter.

5 Stir to obtain a rough dough, then transfer to a floured surface and knead until smooth and elastic. Return to the bowl, cover, and leave to rise in a warm place until doubled in volume, about 2 hours.

6 Grease a large baking sheet. Punch down the dough and knead briefly. Cut the dough in half and form each half into log-shaped loaves.

7 ▼ Place the loaves on the baking sheet and score the tops with a sharp knife. Cover with a clean dish towel, and leave to rise in a warm place until almost doubled, about 50 minutes.

8 Preheat the oven to 375°F.

9 Brush the loaves with the glaze. Bake until the bottoms sound hollow when tapped, 50–55 minutes. If the tops brown too quickly, protect with a sheet of foil. Cool on a rack.

Whole-Wheat Buttermilk Rolls

MAKES 12

2 teaspoons active dry yeast

¼ cup lukewarm water

1 teaspoon sugar

¾ cup lukewarm buttermilk

¼ teaspoon baking soda

1 teaspoon salt

3 tablespoons butter, at room temperature

1½ cups whole-wheat flour

1 cup all-purpose flour

1 beaten egg, for glazing

1 In a large bowl, combine the yeast, water, and sugar. Stir, and leave for 15 minutes to dissolve.

2 ▲ Add the buttermilk, baking soda, salt, and butter and stir to blend. Stir in the whole-wheat flour.

3 Add just enough of the all-purpose flour to obtain a rough dough. If the dough is stiff, stir with your hands.

4 Transfer to a floured surface and knead until smooth and elastic. Divide into 3 equal parts. Roll each into a cylinder, then cut in 4.

5 ▼ Form the pieces into torpedo shapes. Place on a greased baking sheet, cover, and leave in a warm place until doubled in volume.

6 Preheat the oven to 400°F. Brush with the glaze. Bake until firm, 15–20 minutes. Cool on a rack.

French Bread

MAKES 2 LOAVES

1 package active dry yeast

2 cups lukewarm water

1 tablespoon salt

6–8 cups flour

cornmeal, for sprinkling

1 Combine the yeast and water, stir, and leave for 15 minutes to dissolve. Stir in the salt.

2 Add the flour, 1 cup at a time. Beat in with a wooden spoon, adding just enough flour to obtain a smooth dough. Alternatively, use an electric mixer with a dough hook attachment.

3 Transfer to a floured surface and knead until smooth and elastic.

4 Shape into a ball, place in a greased bowl, and cover with a plastic bag. Leave to rise in a warm place until doubled in volume, 2–4 hours.

5 ▲ Transfer to a lightly floured board and shape into two long loaves. Place on a baking sheet sprinkled with cornmeal, let rise for 5 minutes.

6 ▲ Score the tops in several places with a very sharp knife. Brush with water and place in a cold oven. Set a pan of boiling water on the bottom of the oven and set the oven to 400°F. Bake until crusty and golden, about 40 minutes. Cool on a rack.

Whole-Wheat Buttermilk Rolls (top), French Bread

Parker House Rolls

MAKES 48 ROLLS

1 package active dry yeast
2 cups lukewarm milk
½ cup margarine
5 tablespoons sugar
2 teaspoons salt
2 eggs
7–8 cups flour
4 tablespoons butter

1 Combine the yeast and ½ cup milk in a large bowl. Stir and leave for 15 minutes to dissolve.

2 Bring the remaining milk to a simmer, cool for 5 minutes, then beat in the margarine, sugar, salt, and eggs. Let cool to lukewarm.

3 ▲ Pour the milk mixture into the yeast mixture. Stir in 4 cups of flour with a wooden spoon. Add the remaining flour, 1 cup at a time, until a rough dough is obtained.

4 Transfer the dough to a lightly floured surface and knead until smooth and elastic. Place in a clean bowl, cover with a plastic bag, and leave to rise in a warm place until doubled in volume, about 2 hours.

5 In a saucepan, melt the butter and set aside. Grease 2 baking sheets.

6 Punch down the dough and divide into 4 equal pieces. Roll each piece into an 8- × 12-inch rectangle, about ¼ inch thick.

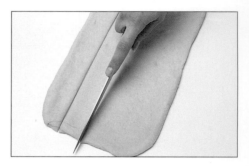

7 ▲ Cut each of the rectangles into 4 2- × 12-inch strips. Cut each strip into 3 4- × 2-inch rectangles.

8 ▲ Brush each rectangle with melted butter, then fold the rectangles in half, so that the top extends about ½ inch over the bottom.

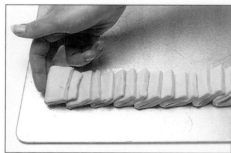

9 ▲ Place the rolls slightly overlapping on the baking sheet, with the longer side facing up.

10 Cover and refrigerate for 30 minutes. Preheat the oven to 350°F. Bake until golden, 18–20 minutes. Cool the rolls slightly before serving.

Clover Leaf Rolls

MAKES 24

1¼ cups milk

2 tablespoons sugar

4 tablespoons butter, at room temperature,

2 teaspoons active dry yeast

1 egg

2 teaspoons salt

3½–4 cups flour

melted butter, for glazing

4 Grease 2 12-cup muffin pans.

5 ▼ Punch down the dough. Cut into 4 equal pieces. Roll each piece into a rope 14 inches long. Cut each rope into 18 pieces, then roll each into a ball.

6 ▲ Place 3 balls, side by side, in each muffin cup. Cover loosely and leave to rise in a warm place until doubled in volume, about 1½ hours.

7 Preheat the oven to 400°F.

8 Brush with glaze. Bake until lightly browned, about 20 minutes. Cool slightly before serving.

1 ▲ Heat the milk until lukewarm; test the temperature with your knuckle. Pour into a large bowl, and stir in the sugar, butter, and yeast. Leave for 15 minutes to dissolve.

2 Stir the egg and salt into the yeast mixture. Gradually stir in 3½ cups of the flour. Add just enough extra flour to obtain a rough dough.

3 ▲ Transfer to a floured surface and knead until smooth and elastic. Place in a greased bowl, cover, and leave in a warm place until doubled in volume, about 1½ hours.

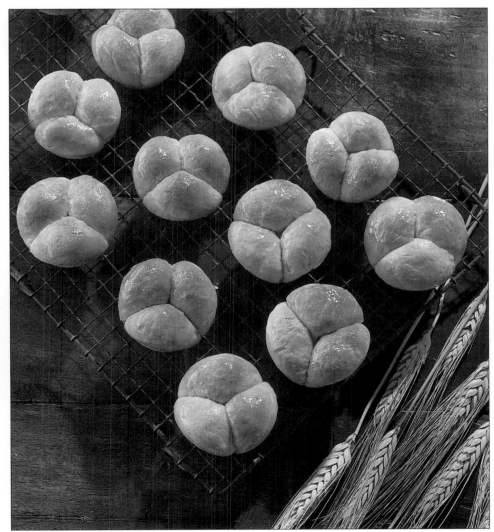

Butter-Poppy Seed Knots

MAKES 12

1¼ cups lukewarm milk

4 tablespoons butter, at room
  temperature

1 teaspoon sugar

2 teaspoons active dry yeast

1 egg yolk

2 teaspoons salt

3½–4 cups flour

1 egg beaten with 2 teaspoons of water,
  for glazing

poppy seeds, for sprinkling

1 In a large bowl, stir together the
milk, butter, sugar, and yeast. Leave
for 15 minutes to dissolve.

2 Stir in the egg yolk, salt, and 2 cups
flour. Add 1 cup of flour and stir to
obtain a soft dough.

3 Transfer to a floured surface and
knead, adding flour if necessary, until
smooth and elastic. Place in a bowl,
cover, and leave in a warm place until
doubled in volume, 1½–2 hours.

4 ▲ Grease a baking sheet. Punch
down the dough with your fist and cut
into 12 pieces the size of golf balls.

5 ▲ Roll each piece to a rope, twist
to form a knot and place 1 inch apart
on the baking sheet. Cover loosely
and leave to rise in a warm place until
doubled in volume, 1–1½ hours.

6 Preheat the oven to 350°F.

7 ▲ Brush the knots with the egg
glaze and sprinkle over the poppy
seeds. Bake until the tops are lightly
browned, 25–30 minutes. Cool
slightly on a rack before serving.

Bread Sticks

MAKES 18–20

1 package active dry yeast
1¼ cups lukewarm water
3 cups flour
2 teaspoons salt
1 teaspoon sugar
2 tablespoons olive oil
1 cup sesame seeds
1 beaten egg, for glazing
coarse salt, for sprinkling

1 Combine the yeast and water, stir, and leave for 15 minutes to dissolve.

2 ▲ Place the flour, salt, sugar, and olive oil in a food processor. With the motor running, slowly pour in the yeast mixture and process until the dough forms a ball. If sticky, add more flour; if dry, add more water.

3 Transfer to a floured surface and knead until smooth and elastic. Place in a bowl, cover, and leave to rise in a warm place for 45 minutes.

4 ▲ Lightly toast the sesame seeds in a skillet. Grease 2 baking sheets.

5 ▼ Roll small handfuls of dough into cylinders, about 12 inches long. Place on the baking sheets.

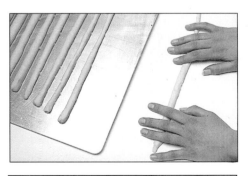

~ VARIATION ~

If preferred, use other seeds, such as poppy or caraway, or for plain bread sticks, omit the seeds and salt.

6 ▲ Brush with egg glaze, sprinkle with the sesame seeds, then sprinkle over some coarse salt. Leave to rise, uncovered, until almost doubled in volume, about 20 minutes.

7 Preheat the oven to 400°F. Bake until golden, about 15 minutes. Turn off the heat but leave the bread sticks in the oven for 5 minutes more. Serve warm or cool.

Croissants

MAKES 18

1 package active dry yeast
1⅓ cups lukewarm milk
2 teaspoons sugar
1½ teaspoons salt
3–3½ cups flour
1 cup (2 sticks) cold unsalted butter
1 egg beaten with 2 teaspoons water, for glazing

1 In the large bowl of an electric mixer, stir together the yeast and warm milk. Leave for 15 minutes to dissolve. Stir in the sugar, salt, and 1 cup of the flour.

2 Using a dough hook, on low speed, gradually add the remaining 2 cups flour. Beat on high until the dough pulls away from the sides of the bowl. Cover and let rise in a warm place until doubled, about 1½ hours.

3 On a lightly floured surface, knead the dough until smooth. Wrap in wax paper and refrigerate for 15 minutes.

4 ▲ Place each ½ cup (1 stick) butter between two sheets of wax paper. With a rolling pin, flatten each to form a 6- × 4-inch rectangle. Set aside.

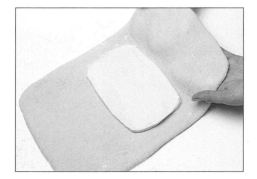

5 ▲ On a floured surface, roll out the dough to a 12- × 8-inch rectangle. Place a butter rectangle in the center. Fold the bottom third of dough over the butter and press gently to seal. Top with the other butter rectangle, then fold over the top dough third.

6 ▲ Turn the dough so that the short side is facing you, with the long folded edge on the left and the long open edge on the right, like a book.

7 Roll the dough gently and evenly into a 12- × 8-inch rectangle; do not press the butter out. Fold in thirds again and mark one corner with your fingertip to indicate the first turn. Wrap and refrigerate for 30 minutes.

8 Repeat twice more: again position the dough like a book, roll, fold in thirds, mark, wrap, and chill. After the third fold, refrigerate at least 2 hours (or overnight).

9 Roll out the dough to a rectangle about 13 inches wide and ⅛ inch thick. Trim the sides to neaten.

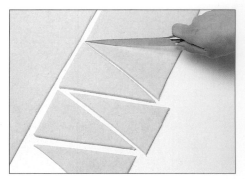

10 ▲ Cut the dough in half lengthwise, then cut into triangles 6 inches high with a 4-inch base.

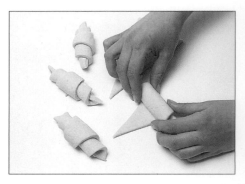

11 ▲ Gently go over the triangles lengthwise with a rolling pin to stretch slightly. Roll up from base to point. Place point-down on baking sheets and curve to form a crescent. Cover and let rise in a warm place until more than doubled in volume, 1–1½ hours. (Or, refrigerate overnight and bake the next day.)

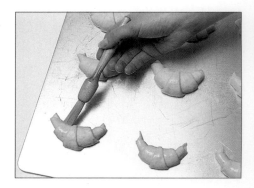

12 ▲ Preheat the oven to 475°F. Brush with the glaze. Bake for 2 minutes. Lower the heat to 375°F and bake until golden, 10–12 more minutes. Cool slightly before serving.

Dill Bread

MAKES 2 LOAVES

4 teaspoons active dry yeast

2 cups lukewarm water

2 tablespoons sugar

7½ cups flour

½ onion, chopped

4 tablespoons oil

l large bunch of dill, finely chopped

2 eggs, lightly beaten

½ cup cottage cheese

4 teaspoons salt

milk, for glazing

1 Mix together the yeast, water, and sugar in a large bowl and leave for 15 minutes to dissolve.

2 ▼ Stir in 3 cups of the flour. Cover and leave to rise in a warm place for 45 minutes.

3 ▲ In a skillet, cook the onion in 1 tablespoon of the oil until soft. Set aside to cool, then stir into the yeast mixture. Stir the dill, eggs, cottage cheese, salt, and remaining oil into the yeast mixture. Gradually add the remaining flour until too stiff to stir.

4 ▲ Transfer to a floured surface and knead until smooth and elastic. Place in a bowl, cover, and leave to rise until doubled in volume, 1–1½ hours.

5 ▲ Grease a large baking sheet. Cut the dough in half and shape into 2 rounds. Leave to rise in a warm place for 30 minutes.

6 Preheat the oven to 375°F. Score the tops, brush with the milk, and bake until browned, about 50 minutes. Cool on a rack.

Spiral Herb Bread

MAKES 2 LOAVES

2 packages active dry yeast
2½ cups lukewarm water
3 cups all-purpose flour
3 cups whole-wheat flour
3 teaspoons salt
2 tablespoons butter
1 large bunch of parsley, finely chopped
1 bunch of scallions, finely chopped
1 garlic clove, finely chopped
salt and freshly ground black pepper
1 egg, lightly beaten
milk, for glazing

1 Combine the yeast and ¼ cup of the water, stir, and leave for 15 minutes to dissolve.

2 Combine the flours and salt in a large bowl. Make a well in the center and pour in the yeast mixture and the remaining water. With a wooden spoon, stir from the center, working outwards to obtain a rough dough.

3 Transfer the dough to a floured surface and knead until smooth and elastic. Return to the bowl, cover with a plastic bag, and leave until doubled in volume, about 2 hours.

4 ▲ Meanwhile, combine the butter, parsley, scallions, and garlic in a large skillet. Cook over low heat, stirring, until softened. Season with salt and pepper and set aside.

5 Grease 2 9- × 5-inch bread pans. When the dough has risen, cut it in half, then roll each half into a rectangle about 14 × 9 inches.

6 ▼ Brush both with the beaten egg. Divide the herb mixture between the two, spreading just up to the edges.

7 ▲ Roll up to enclose the filling and pinch the short ends to seal. Place in the pans, seam-side down. Cover, and leave in a warm place until the dough rises above the rim of the pans.

8 Preheat the oven to 375°F. Brush with milk and bake until the bottoms sound hollow when tapped, about 55 minutes. Cool on a rack.

Pizza

MAKES 2

3½ cups flour
1 teaspoon salt
2 teaspoons active dry yeast
1¼ cups lukewarm water
¼–½ cup extra-virgin olive oil
tomato sauce, grated cheese, olives, and herbs, for topping

1 Combine the flour and salt in a large mixing bowl. Make a well in the center and add the yeast, water, and 2 tablespoons of the olive oil. Leave for 15 minutes to dissolve the yeast.

2 With your hands, stir until the dough just holds together. Transfer to a floured surface and knead until smooth and elastic. Avoid adding too much flour while kneading.

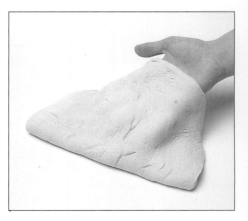

3 ▲ Brush the inside of a clean bowl with 1 tablespoon of the oil. Place the dough in the bowl and roll around to coat with the oil. Cover with a plastic bag and leave to rise in a warm place until more than doubled in volume, about 45 minutes.

4 Divide the dough into 2 balls. Preheat the oven to 400°F.

5 ▲ Roll each ball into a 10-inch circle. Flip the circles over and onto your palm. Set each circle on the work surface and rotate, stretching the dough as you turn, until it is about 12 inches in diameter.

6 ▲ Brush 2 pizza pans with oil. Place the dough circles in the pans and neaten the edges. Brush with oil.

7 ▲ Cover with the toppings and bake until golden, 10–12 minutes.

Cheese Bread

MAKES 1 LOAF

1 package active dry yeast
1 cup lukewarm milk
2 tablespoons butter
3 cups flour
2 teaspoon salt
1 cup grated sharp cheddar cheese

1 Combine the yeast and milk, stir, and leave for 15 minutes to dissolve.

2 Melt the butter, let cool, and add to the yeast mixture.

3 Mix the flour and salt together in a large bowl. Make a well in the center and pour in the yeast mixture.

4 With a wooden spoon, stir from the center, incorporating flour with each turn, to obtain a rough dough. If the dough seems too dry, add 2–3 tablespoons water.

5 Transfer to a floured surface and knead until smooth and elastic. Return to the bowl, cover, and leave to rise in a warm place until doubled in volume, 2–3 hours.

6 ▲ Grease a 9- × 5-inch bread pan. Punch down the dough with your fist. Knead in the cheese, distributing it as evenly as possible.

7 ▼ Twist the dough, form into a loaf shape and place in the pan, tucking the ends under. Leave in a warm place until the dough rises above the rim of the pan.

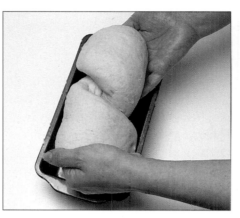

8 ▲ Preheat the oven to 400°F. Bake for 15 minutes, then lower the heat to 375°F and bake until the bottom sounds hollow when tapped, about 30 minutes more. Cool on a rack.

Italian Flat Bread With Sage

MAKES 1 LOAF

1 package active dry yeast
1 cup lukewarm water
3 cups flour
2 teaspoons salt
5 tablespoons extra-virgin olive oil
12 fresh sage leaves, chopped

1 Combine the yeast and water, stir, and leave for 15 minutes to dissolve.

2 Mix the flour and salt in a large bowl and make a well in the center.

3 Stir in the yeast mixture and 4 tablespoons of the oil. Stir from the center, incorporating flour with each turn, to obtain a rough dough.

4 ▲ Transfer to a floured surface and knead until smooth and elastic. Place in a lightly oiled bowl. Cover and leave to rise in a warm place until doubled in volume, about 2 hours.

5 Preheat the oven to 400°F and place a baking sheet in the center of the oven.

6 Punch down the dough. Knead in the sage leaves, then roll to a 12-inch circle. Leave to rise slightly.

7 ▼ Dimple the surface all over with your finger. Drizzle the remaining oil on top. Slide a floured board under the bread, carry to the oven, and slide off onto the hot baking sheet. Bake until golden brown, about 35 minutes. Cool on a rack.

Zucchini Yeast Bread

MAKES 1 LOAF

1 pound zucchini, grated
2 tablespoons salt
1 package active dry yeast
1¼ cups lukewarm water
3½ cups flour
olive oil, for brushing

1 ▼ In a colander, alternate layers of grated zucchini and salt. Leave for 30 minutes, then squeeze out the moisture with your hands.

2 Combine the yeast with ¼ cup of lukewarm water, stir, and leave for 15 minutes to dissolve the yeast.

3 ▲ Place the zucchini, yeast, and flour in a bowl. Stir together, and add just enough of the remaining water to obtain a rough dough.

4 Transfer to a floured surface and knead until smooth and elastic. Return the dough to the bowl, cover with a plastic bag, and leave to rise in a warm place until doubled in volume, about 1½ hours.

5 Grease a baking sheet. Punch down the risen dough with your fist and knead into a tapered cylinder. Place on the baking sheet, cover, and leave to rise in a warm place until doubled in volume, about 45 minutes.

6 ▼ Preheat the oven to 425°F. Brush with olive oil and bake until golden, 40–45 minutes. Cool on a rack.

Italian Flat Bread with Sage (top), Zucchini Yeast Bread

Olive Bread

MAKES 2 LOAVES

4 teaspoons active dry yeast
2 cups warm water
3½ cups all-purpose flour
1½ cups whole-wheat flour
½ cup cornmeal
2 teaspoons salt
2 tablespoons olive oil
1 cup pitted mixed green and black olives, cut in half
cornmeal, for sprinkling

1 Combine the yeast and water, stir, and leave for 5 minutes to dissolve.

2 Stir in 2 cups of the all-purpose flour, cover, and leave in a warm place for 1 hour.

3 In a large mixing bowl, combine the remaining all-purpose flour, whole-wheat flour, cornmeal, and salt. Make a well in the center; pour in the olive oil and yeast mixture.

4 ▼ With a wooden spoon, stir from the center, incorporating flour with each turn. When the dough becomes too stiff, stir with your hands until a rough dough is obtained.

5 Transfer to a floured surface and knead until smooth and elastic. Return to the bowl, cover, and leave to rise in a warm place until doubled in volume, about 1½ hours.

6 ▲ Punch down the dough with your fist. Add the olives and knead in as evenly as possible.

7 Cut the dough in half and shape each half into a round. Sprinkle a baking sheet with cornmeal. Place the rounds on the sheet, seam-side down. Cover with a dish towel and leave to rise until nearly doubled in volume.

8 Place a baking pan in the bottom of the oven and half fill with hot water. Preheat the oven to 425°F.

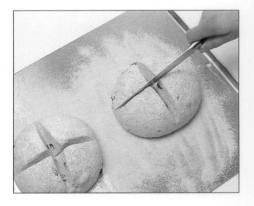

9 ▲ With a sharp knife, score the tops of the loaves.

10 Bake for 20 minutes. Lower the heat to 375°F and bake until the bottoms sound hollow when tapped, 25–30 minutes more. Cool on a rack.

Pumpkin Spice Bread

MAKES 1 LOAF

2 packages active dry yeast
1 cup lukewarm water
2 teaspoons ground cinnamon
1 teaspoon ground ginger
1 teaspoon ground allspice
¼ teaspoon ground cloves
1 teaspoon salt
½ cup instant nonfat dry milk
1 cup cooked or canned pumpkin
1¼ cups sugar
½ cup (1 stick) butter, melted
5½ cups flour
½ cup pecans, finely chopped

1 In the bowl of an electric mixer, combine the yeast and water, stir, and leave for 15 minutes to dissolve. In another bowl, mix the spices together and set aside.

2 To the yeast, add the salt, milk, pumpkin, ½ cup of the sugar, 3 tablespoons butter, 2 teaspoons of the spice mixture, and 2 cups of the flour.

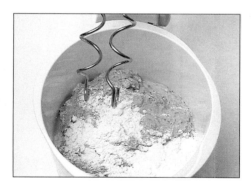

3 ▲ With the dough hook, mix on low speed until blended. Gradually add the remaining flour and mix on medium speed until a rough dough is formed. Alternatively, mix by hand.

4 Transfer to a floured surface and knead until smooth. Place in a bowl, cover, and leave to rise in a warm place until doubled, 1–1½ hours.

5 ▼ Punch down and knead briefly. Divide the dough into thirds. Roll each third into an 18-inch long rope. Cut each rope into 18 equal pieces, then roll into balls.

6 Grease a 10-inch tube pan. Stir the remaining sugar into the remaining spice mixture. Roll the balls in the remaining melted butter, then in the sugar and spice mixture.

7 ▲ Place 18 balls in the pan and sprinkle over half the pecans. Add the remaining balls, staggering the rows, and sprinkle over the remaining pecans. Cover with a plastic bag and leave to rise in a warm place until almost doubled, about 45 minutes.

8 Preheat the oven to 350°F. Bake for 55 minutes. Cool in the pan for 20 minutes, then unmold. Serve warm.

Walnut Bread

Makes 1 loaf

2½ cups whole-wheat flour

1 cup all-purpose flour

2½ teaspoons salt

2¼ cups lukewarm water

1 tablespoon honey

1 package active dry yeast

1¼ cup walnut pieces, plus more for decorating

1 beaten egg, for glazing

1   Combine the flours and salt in a large bowl. Make a well in the center and add 1 cup of the water, the honey and the yeast.

2   Set aside until the yeast dissolves and the mixture is frothy.

3   Add the remaining water. With a wooden spoon, stir from the center, incorporating flour with each turn, to obtain a smooth dough. Add more flour if the dough is too sticky and use your hands if the dough becomes too stiff to stir.

4   Transfer to a floured board and knead, adding flour if necessary, until the dough is smooth and elastic. Place in a greased bowl and roll the dough around in the bowl to coat thoroughly on all sides.

5 ▲   Cover with a plastic bag and leave in a warm place until doubled in volume, about 1½ hours.

6 ▲   Punch down the dough and knead in the walnuts evenly.

7   Grease a baking sheet. Shape into a round loaf and place on the baking sheet. Press in walnut pieces to decorate the top. Cover loosely with a damp cloth and leave to rise in a warm place until doubled, 25–30 minutes.

8   Preheat the oven to 425°F.

9 ▲   With a sharp knife, score the top. Brush with the glaze. Bake for 15 minutes. Lower the heat to 375°F and bake until the bottom sounds hollow when tapped, about 40 minutes. Cool on a rack.

Pecan Rye Bread

MAKES 2 LOAVES

1½ packages active dry yeast
3 cups lukewarm water
5 cups all-purpose flour
3 cups rye flour
2 tablespoons salt
1 tablespoon honey
2 teaspoons caraway seeds, (optional)
½ cup (1 stick) butter, at room temperature
2 cups pecans, chopped

1 Combine the yeast and ½ cup of the water. Stir and leave for 15 minutes to dissolve.

2 In the bowl of an electric mixer, combine the flours, salt, honey, caraway seeds, and butter. With the dough hook, mix on low speed until well blended.

3 Add the yeast mixture and the remaining water and mix on medium speed until the dough forms a ball.

4 ▲ Transfer to a floured surface and knead in the pecans.

5 Return the dough to a clean bowl, cover with a plastic bag, and leave in a warm place until doubled in volume, about 2 hours.

6 Grease 2 8½- × 4½-inch bread pans.

7 ▲ Punch down the risen dough.

8 Divide the dough in half and form into loaves. Place in the pans, seam-side down. Dust the tops with flour.

9 Cover with plastic bags and leave to rise in a warm place until doubled in volume, about 1 hour.

10 Preheat the oven to 375°F.

11 ▼ Bake until the bottoms sound hollow when tapped, 45–50 minutes. Cool on racks.

Sticky Buns

MAKES 18

⅔ cup milk
1 package active dry yeast
2 tablespoons granulated sugar
3–3¼ cups flour
1 teaspoon salt
½ cup (1 stick) cold butter, cut in pieces
2 eggs, lightly beaten
grated rind of 1 lemon
FOR THE TOPPING AND FILLING
1¼ cups dark brown sugar, firmly packed
5 tablespoons butter
½ cup water
¾ cup pecans, chopped
3 tablespoons granulated sugar
2 teaspoons ground cinnamon
¾ cup raisins

1 Heat the milk to lukewarm. Add the yeast and sugar and leave until frothy, about 15 minutes.

2 Combine the flour and salt in a large mixing bowl. Add the butter and cut in with a pastry blender until the mixture resembles coarse crumbs.

3 ▲ Make a well in the center and add the yeast mixture, eggs, and lemon rind. With a wooden spoon, stir from the center, incorporating flour with each turn. When it becomes too stiff, stir by hand to obtain a rough dough.

4 Transfer to a floured surface and knead until smooth and elastic. Return to the bowl, cover with a plastic bag, and leave to rise in a warm place until doubled in volume, about 2 hours.

5 Meanwhile, for the topping, make the syrup. Combine the brown sugar, butter, and water in a heavy saucepan. Bring to a boil and boil gently until thick and syrupy, about 10 minutes.

6 ▲ Place 1 tablespoon of the syrup in the bottom of each of 18 1½-inch muffin cups. Sprinkle in a thin layer of chopped pecans, reserving the rest for the filling.

7 Punch down the dough and transfer to a floured surface. Roll out to an 18- × 12-inch rectangle.

8 ▲ For the filling, combine the granulated sugar, cinnamon, raisins, and reserved nuts. Sprinkle over the dough in an even layer.

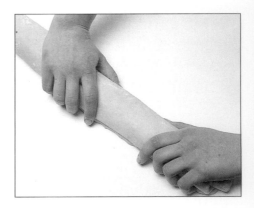

9 ▲ Roll up tightly, from the long side, to form a cylinder.

10 ▲ Cut the cylinder into 1-inch rounds. Place each in a prepared muffin cup, cut-side up. Leave to rise in a warm place until increased by half, about 30 minutes.

11 Preheat the oven to 350°F. Place a sheet of foil under the pans to catch any syrup that bubbles over. Bake until golden, about 25 minutes.

12 Remove from the oven and invert the pans onto a sheet of wax paper. Leave for 3–5 minutes, then remove buns from the pans. Transfer to a rack to cool. Serve sticky-side up.

~ COOK'S TIP ~

To save time and energy, make double the recipe and freeze half for another occasion.

Raisin Bread

MAKES 2 LOAVES

1 package active dry yeast
2 cups lukewarm milk
1 cup raisins
½ cup currants
1 tablespoon sherry or brandy
½ teaspoon grated nutmeg
grated rind of 1 large orange
⅓ cup sugar
1 tablespoon salt
8 tablespoons butter, melted
5–6 cups flour
1 egg beaten with 1 tablespoon cream, for glazing

1 Stir together the yeast and ½ cup of the milk and let stand for 15 minutes to dissolve.

2 ▲ Mix the raisins, currants, sherry or brandy, nutmeg and orange rind together and set aside.

3 In another bowl, mix the remaining milk, sugar, salt and 4 tablespoons of the butter. Add the yeast mixture. With a wooden spoon, stir in 2–3 cups flour, 1 cup at a time, until blended. Add the remaining flour as needed for a stiff dough.

4 Transfer to a floured surface and knead until smooth and elastic. Place in a greased bowl, cover, and leave to rise in a warm place until doubled in volume, about 2½ hours.

5 Punch down the dough, return to the bowl, cover, and leave to rise in a warm place for 30 minutes.

6 Grease 2 8½- × 4½- inch bread pans. Divide the dough in half and roll each half into a rectangle about 20 × 7 inches.

7 ▲ Brush the rectangles with the remaining melted butter. Sprinkle over the raisin mixture, then roll up tightly, tucking in the ends slightly as you roll. Place in the prepared pans, cover, and leave to rise until almost doubled in volume.

8 ▲ Preheat the oven to 400°F. Brush the top of the loaves with the glaze. Bake for 20 minutes. Lower the heat to 350°F and bake until golden, 25–30 minutes more. Cool on racks.

Prune Bread

MAKES 1 LOAF

1 cup dried prunes

1 package active dry yeast

½ cup whole-wheat flour

2½–3 cups all-purpose flour

½ teaspoon baking soda

1 teaspoon salt

1 teaspoon pepper

2 tablespoons butter, at room temperature

¾ cup buttermilk

½ cup walnuts, chopped

milk, for glazing

1 Simmer the prunes in water to cover until soft, or soak overnight. Drain, reserving ¼ cup of the soaking liquid. Pit and chop the prunes.

2 Combine the yeast and the reserved prune liquid, stir, and leave for 15 minutes to dissolve.

3 In a large bowl, stir together the flours, baking soda, salt, and pepper. Make a well in the center.

4 ▲ Add the chopped prunes, butter, and buttermilk. Pour in the yeast mixture. With a wooden spoon, stir from the center, incorporating more flour with each turn, to obtain a rough dough.

5 Transfer to a floured surface and knead until smooth and elastic. Return to the bowl, cover with a plastic bag, and leave to rise in a warm place until doubled in volume, about 1½ hours.

6 Grease a baking sheet.

7 ▲ Punch down the dough with your fist, then knead in the walnuts.

8 Shape the dough into a long, cylindrical loaf. Place on the baking sheet, cover loosely, and leave to rise in a warm place for 45 minutes.

9 Preheat the oven to 425°F.

10 ▼ With a sharp knife, score the top deeply. Brush with milk and bake for 15 minutes. Lower the heat to 375°F and bake until the bottom sounds hollow when tapped, about 35 minutes more. Cool on a rack.

Prune-Filled Coffee Cake

MAKES 1 LOAF

1 package active dry yeast
¼ cup lukewarm water
¼ cup lukewarm milk
¼ cup sugar
½ teaspoon salt
1 egg
4 tablespoons butter, at room temperature
3–3½ cups flour
1 egg beaten with 2 teaspoons water, for glazing

FOR THE FILLING

1 cup cooked prunes
2 teaspoons grated lemon rind
1 teaspoon grated orange rind
¼ teaspoon freshly grated nutmeg
3 tablespoons butter, melted
½ cup walnuts, very finely chopped
2 tablespoons sugar

1 In a large bowl, combine the yeast and water, stir, and leave for 15 minutes to dissolve.

2 Stir in the milk, sugar, salt, egg, and butter. Gradually stir in 2½ cups of the flour to obtain a soft dough.

3 Transfer to a floured surface and knead in just enough flour to obtain a dough that is smooth and elastic. Put into a clean bowl, cover, and leave to rise in a warm place until doubled in volume, about 1½ hours.

~ **VARIATION** ~

For Apricot-Filled Coffee Cake, replace the prunes with the same amount of dried apricots. It is not necessary to cook them, but to soften, soak them in hot tea and discard the liquid before using.

4 ▲ Meanwhile, for the filling, combine the prunes, lemon and orange rinds, nutmeg, butter, walnuts, and sugar and stir to blend. Set aside.

5 Grease a large baking sheet. Punch down the dough and transfer to a lightly floured surface. Knead briefly, then roll out into a 15- × 10-inch rectangle. Carefully transfer to the baking sheet.

6 ▲ Spread the filling in the center.

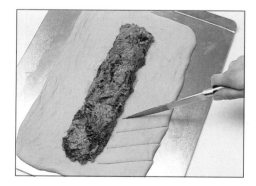

7 ▲ With a sharp knife, cut 10 strips at an angle on either side of the filling, cutting just to the filling.

8 ▲ For a braided pattern, fold up one end neatly, then fold over the strips from alternating sides until all the strips are folded over. Tuck excess dough at ends underneath.

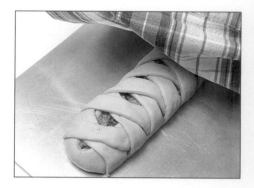

9 ▲ Cover loosely with a dish towel and leave to rise in a warm place until almost doubled in volume.

10 ▲ Preheat the oven to 375°F. Brush with the glaze. Bake until browned, about 30 minutes. Transfer to a rack to cool.

Kugelhopf

MAKES 1 LOAF

¾ cup raisins

1 tablespoon kirsch or brandy

1 package active dry yeast

¼ cup lukewarm water

½ cup (1 stick) unsalted butter, at room temperature

½ cup sugar

3 eggs, at room temperature

grated rind of 1 lemon

1 teaspoon salt

½ teaspoon vanilla extract

3 cups flour

½ cup milk

¼ cup slivered almonds

½ cup blanched almonds, chopped

confectioners' sugar, for dusting

1 ▼ In a bowl, combine the raisins and kirsch or brandy. Set aside.

2 Combine the yeast and water, stir, and leave for 15 minutes to dissolve.

3 With an electric mixer, cream the butter and sugar until thick and fluffy. Beat in the eggs, one at a time. Add the lemon rind, salt, and vanilla. Stir in the yeast mixture.

4 ▲ Add the flour, alternating with the milk, until the mixture is well blended. Cover and leave to rise in a warm place until doubled in volume, about 2 hours.

5 ▲ Grease a 10-cup kugelhopf mold, then sprinkle the slivered almonds evenly over the bottom.

6 Work the raisins and almonds into the dough, then spoon into the mold. Cover with a plastic bag, and leave to rise in a warm place until the dough almost reaches the top of the pan, about 1 hour.

7 Preheat the oven to 350°F.

8 Bake until golden brown, about 45 minutes. If the top browns too quickly, protect with a sheet of foil. Let cool in the pan for 15 minutes, then invert onto a rack. Dust the top lightly with confectioners' sugar before serving.

Panettone

MAKES 1 LOAF

⅔ cup lukewarm milk
1 package active dry yeast
3–3½ cups flour
⅓ cup sugar
2 teaspoons salt
2 eggs
5 egg yolks
¾ cup (1½ sticks) unsalted butter, at room temperature
¾ cup raisins
grated rind of 1 lemon
½ cup candied citrus peel, chopped

1 Combine the milk and yeast in a large warmed bowl and leave for 10 minutes to dissolve.

2 Stir in 1 cup of the flour, cover loosely, and leave in a warm place for 30 minutes.

3 Sift over the remaining flour. Make a well in the center and add the sugar, salt, eggs, and egg yolks.

4 ▲ Stir with a wooden spoon until too stiff, then stir with your hands to obtain a very elastic and sticky dough. Add a little more flour if necessary, but keep the dough as soft as possible.

5 ▲ To incorporate the butter, smear over the butter, then work it in with your hands. When evenly distributed, cover, and leave to rise in a warm place until doubled in volume, 3–4 hours.

6 Line the bottom of an 8-cup charlotte mold or 2-pound coffee can with wax paper, then grease the bottom and sides.

7 Punch down the dough and transfer to a floured surface. Knead in the raisins, lemon rind, and citrus peel.

8 ▲ Transfer the dough to the mold. Cover with a plastic bag and leave to rise until the dough is well above the top of the container, about 2 hours.

9 Preheat the oven to 400°F. Bake for 15 minutes, cover the top with foil, and lower the heat to 350°F. Bake 30 minutes more. Let cool in the mold 5 minutes, then transfer to a rack.

Danish Wreath

SERVES 10–12

1 package active dry yeast
½ cup lukewarm milk
2½ cups flour
¼ cup granulated sugar
1 teaspoon salt
½ teaspoon vanilla extract
1 egg, beaten
1 cup (2 sticks) unsalted butter
1 egg yolk beaten with 2 teaspoons water, for glazing
1 cup confectioners' sugar
1–2 tablespoons water
chopped pecans, for sprinkling
FOR THE FILLING
1 cup dark brown sugar, firmly packed
1 teaspoon ground cinnamon
½ cup pecans, toasted and chopped
1 tablespoon egg white, beaten

1 Combine the yeast and milk, stir, and leave for 15 minutes to dissolve.

2 Combine the flour, sugar, and salt. Make a well in the center and add the yeast mixture, vanilla, and egg. Stir until a rough dough is formed.

3 Transfer to a floured surface and knead until smooth and elastic. Wrap and refrigerate for 15 minutes.

~ **VARIATION** ~

For a different filling, substitute
3 tart apples, peeled and grated,
the grated rind of 1 lemon,
1 tablespoon lemon juice,
½ teaspoon ground cinnamon,
3 tablespoons sugar, ¼ cup
currants, and ¼ cup chopped
walnuts. Combine well and use
as described.

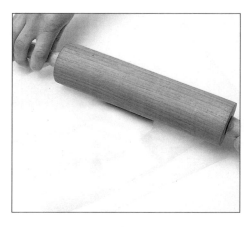

4 ▲ Meanwhile, place each ½ cup (1 stick) butter between two sheets of wax paper. With a rolling pin, flatten each to form 2 6- × 4-inch rectangles. Set aside.

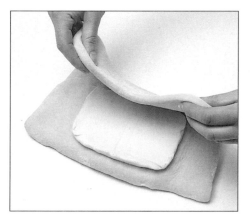

5 ▲ Roll out the dough to a 12- × 8-inch rectangle. Place one butter rectangle in the center. Fold the bottom third of dough over the butter and seal the edge to enclose it. Place the other butter rectangle on top and cover with the top third of the dough.

6 Turn the dough so the shorter side faces you. Roll into an 12- × 8-inch rectangle. Fold into thirds, and indent one edge with your finger to indicate the first turn. Wrap in wax paper and refrigerate for 30 minutes.

7 Repeat two more times; rolling, folding, marking and chilling between each turn. After the third fold refrigerate for 1–2 hours, or longer.

8 Grease a large baking sheet. In a bowl, stir together all the filling ingredients until blended.

9 ▲ Roll out the dough to a 25- × 6-inch strip. Spread over a thin layer of filling, leaving a ½-inch border.

10 Roll up the dough lengthwise into a cylinder. Place on the baking sheet and form into a circle, pinching the edges together to seal. Cover with an inverted bowl and leave in a warm place to rise for 45 minutes.

11 ▲ Preheat the oven to 400°F. Slash the top every 2 inches, cutting about ½ inch deep. Brush with the glaze. Bake until golden, 35–40 minutes. Cool on a rack. To serve, mix the confectioners' sugar and water, then drizzle over the wreath. Sprinkle with the pecans.

PIES & TARTS

~

Here is every sort of filling – from orchard fruits to autumn nuts, tangy citrus to luscious chocolate – for the most memorable pies and tarts. Some are plain and some are fancy, but all are delicious.

Plum Pie

SERVES 8

2 pounds red or purple plums

grated rind of 1 lemon

1 tablespoon fresh lemon juice

½–¾ cup sugar

3 tablespoons quick-cooking tapioca

⅛ teaspoon salt

½ teaspoon ground cinnamon

¼ teaspoon grated nutmeg

FOR THE CRUST

2 cups flour

1 teaspoon salt

6 tablespoons cold butter, cut in pieces

4 tablespoons cold shortening, cut in pieces

¼–½ cup ice water

milk, for glazing

1 ▼ For the crust, sift the flour and salt into a bowl. Add the butter and shortening and cut in with a pastry blender until the mixture resembles coarse crumbs.

2 Stir in just enough water to bind the dough. Gather into 2 balls, one slightly larger than the other. Wrap and refrigerate for 20 minutes.

3 Place a baking sheet in the center of the oven and preheat to 425°F.

4 On a lightly floured surface, roll out the larger dough ball about ⅛ inch thick. Transfer to a 9-inch pie pan and trim the edge.

5 ▲ Halve the plums, discard the pits, and cut in large pieces. Mix all the filling ingredients together (if the plums are very tart, use ¾ cup sugar). Transfer to the pie shell.

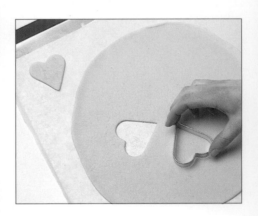

6 ▲ Roll out the remaining dough and place on a baking tray lined with wax paper. Stamp out 4 heart shapes and reserve them. Transfer the dough to the pie using the wax paper.

7 Trim to leave a ¾-inch overhang. Fold the top edge under the bottom and pinch to seal. Arrange the dough hearts on top. Brush with the milk. Bake for 15 minutes. Reduce the heat to 350°F and bake 30–35 minutes more. If the crust browns too quickly, protect with a sheet of foil.

Blueberry Pie

SERVES 8

1 pound blueberries
½ cup sugar
3 tablespoons cornstarch
2 tablespoons fresh lemon juice
2 tablespoons butter, diced

FOR THE CRUST

2 cups flour
¾ teaspoon salt
½ cup (1 stick) cold butter, cut in pieces
3 tablespoons cold shortening, cut in pieces
5–6 tablespoons ice water
1 egg beaten with 1 tablespoon water, for glazing

1 For the crust, sift the flour and salt into a bowl. Add the butter and shortening and cut in with a pastry blender until the mixture resembles coarse crumbs. With a fork, stir in just enough water to bind the dough. Gather into 2 equal balls, wrap in wax paper, and refrigerate for 20 minutes.

2 On a lightly floured surface, roll out one dough ball about ⅛ inch thick. Transfer to a 9-inch pie pan and trim to leave a ½-inch overhang. Brush the bottom with egg glaze.

3 ▲ Mix all the filling ingredients together, except the butter (reserve a few blueberries for decoration). Spoon into the shell and dot with the butter. Brush the egg glaze on the edge of the lower crust.

4 Place a baking sheet in the center of the oven and preheat to 425°F.

5 ▼ Roll out the remaining dough on a baking tray lined with wax paper. With a serrated pastry wheel, cut out 24 thin strips of dough. Roll out the scraps and cut out leaf shapes. Mark veins in the leaves with the point of a knife.

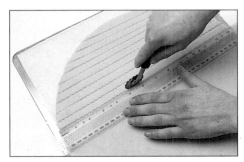

6 ▲ Weave the strips in a close lattice, then transfer to the pie using the wax paper. Press the edges to seal and trim. Arrange the dough leaves around the rim. Brush with egg glaze.

7 Bake for 10 minutes. Reduce the heat to 350°F and bake until the pastry is golden, 40–45 minutes more. Decorate with reserved blueberries.

Raspberry Tart

SERVES 8

4 egg yolks

⅓ cup sugar

3 tablespoons flour

1¼ cups milk

⅛ teaspoon salt

½ teaspoon vanilla extract

1 pound fresh raspberries (about 1 quart)

5 tablespoons concord grape jelly

1 tablespoon fresh orange juice

FOR THE CRUST

1¼ cups flour

½ teaspoon baking powder

¼ teaspoon salt

1 tablespoon sugar

grated rind of ½ orange

6 tablespoons cold butter, cut in pieces

1 egg yolk

3–4 tablespoons whipping cream

1 For the crust, sift the flour, baking powder, and salt into a bowl. Stir in the sugar and orange rind. Add the butter and cut in with a pastry blender until the mixture resembles coarse crumbs. With a fork, stir in the egg yolk and just enough cream to bind the dough. Gather into a ball, wrap in wax paper, and refrigerate.

2 For the custard filling, beat the egg yolks and sugar until thick and lemon-colored..Gradually stir in the flour.

3 In a saucepan, bring the milk and salt just to the boil, and remove from the heat. Whisk into the egg yolk mixture, return to the pan, and continue whisking over moderately high heat until just bubbling. Cook for 3 minutes to thicken. Transfer immediately to a bowl. Add the vanilla and stir to blend.

4 ▲ Cover with wax paper to prevent a skin from forming.

5 ▲ Preheat the oven to 400°F. On a lightly floured surface, roll out the dough about ⅛ inch thick, transfer to a 10-inch tart pan and trim the edge. Prick the bottom all over with a fork and line with crumpled wax paper. Fill with pie weights and bake for 15 minutes. Remove the paper and weights. Continue baking until golden, 6–8 minutes more. Let cool.

6 ▲ Spread an even layer of the pastry cream filling in the tart shell and arrange the raspberries on top. Melt the jelly and orange juice in a pan and brush on top to glaze.

Rhubarb Cherry Pie

SERVES 8

1 pound rhubarb, cut into 1-inch pieces (about 3 cups)

1 1-pound can (2 cups) pitted tart red or black cherries, drained

1¼ cups sugar

¼ cup quick-cooking tapioca

FOR THE CRUST

2 cups flour

1 teaspoon salt

6 tablespoons cold butter, cut in pieces

4 tablespoons cold shortening, cut in pieces

¼–½ cup ice water

milk, for glazing

1 ▲ For the crust, sift the flour and salt into a bowl. Add the butter and shortening to the dry ingredients and cut in with a pastry blender until the mixture resembles coarse crumbs.

2 With a fork, stir in just enough water to bind the dough. Gather the dough into 2 balls, one slightly larger than the other. Wrap the dough in wax paper and refrigerate for at least 20 minutes.

3 Place a baking sheet in the center of the oven and preheat to 400°F.

4 On a lightly floured surface, roll out the larger dough ball to a thickness of about ⅛ inch.

5 ▼ Roll the dough around the rolling pin and transfer to a 9-inch pie pan. Trim the edge to leave a ½-inch overhang all around.

6 Refrigerate the pie shell while making the filling.

7 In a mixing bowl, combine the rhubarb, cherries, sugar, and tapioca and spoon into the pie shell.

8 ▲ Roll out the remaining dough and cut out leaf shapes.

9 Transfer the dough to the pie and trim to leave a ¾-inch overhang. Fold the top edge under the bottom and flute. Roll small balls from the scraps. Mark veins in the dough leaves and place on top with the dough balls.

10 Glaze the top and bake until golden, 40–50 minutes.

Peach Leaf Pie

2½ pounds ripe peaches

juice of 1 lemon

½ cup sugar

3 tablespoons cornstarch

¼ teaspoon grated nutmeg

½ teaspoon ground cinnamon

2 tablespoons butter, diced

FOR THE CRUST

2 cups flour

¾ teaspoon salt

½ cup (1 stick) cold butter, cut in pieces

3 tablespoons cold shortening, cut in pieces

5–6 tablespoons ice water

1 egg beaten with 1 tablespoon water, for glazing

1 For the crust, sift the flour and salt into a bowl. Add the butter and shortening and cut in with a pastry blender until the mixture resembles coarse crumbs.

2 ▲ With a fork, stir in just enough water to bind the dough. Gather into 2 balls, one slightly larger than the other. Wrap in wax paper and refrigerate for at least 20 minutes.

3 Place a baking sheet in the oven and preheat to 425°F.

4 ▲ Drop a few peaches at a time into boiling water for 20 seconds, then transfer to a bowl of cold water. When cool, peel off the skins.

5 Slice the peaches and combine with the lemon juice, sugar, cornstarch, and spices. Set aside.

6 ▲ On a lightly floured surface, roll out the larger dough ball about ⅛ inch thick. Transfer to a 9-inch pie pan and trim the edge. Refrigerate.

7 ▲ Roll out the remaining dough ¼ inch thick. Cut out leaf shapes 3 inches long, using a template if needed. Mark veins with a knife. With the scraps, roll a few balls.

8 ▲ Brush the bottom of the pie shell with egg glaze. Add the peaches, piling them higher in the center. Dot with the butter.

9 ▲ To assemble, start from the outside edge and cover the peaches with a ring of leaves. Place a second ring of leaves above, staggering the positions. Continue with rows of leaves until covered. Place the balls in the center. Brush with glaze.

10 Bake for 10 minutes. Lower the heat to 350°F and continue to bake for 35–40 minutes more.

~ COOK'S TIP ~

Baking the pie on a preheated baking sheet helps to make the bottom crust crisp. The moisture from the filling keeps the bottom crust more humid than the top, but this baking method helps to compensate for the top crust being better exposed to the heat source.

Peach Tart with Almond Cream

SERVES 8–10

4 large ripe freestone peaches

⅔ cup blanched almonds

2 tablespoons flour

7 tablespoons unsalted butter, at room temperature

½ cup plus 2 tablespoons sugar

1 egg

1 egg yolk

½ teaspoon vanilla extract, or 2 teaspoons rum

FOR THE CRUST

1¼ cups flour

¾ teaspoon salt

7 tablespoons cold unsalted butter, cut in pieces

1 egg yolk

2½–3 tablespoons ice water

1 ▲ For the crust, sift the flour and salt into a bowl.

2 Add the butter and cut in with a pastry blender until the mixture resembles coarse crumbs. With a fork, stir in the egg yolk and just enough water to bind the dough. Gather into a ball, wrap in wax paper, and refrigerate for at least 20 minutes.

3 Place a baking sheet in the oven and preheat to 400°F.

4 ▲ On a lightly floured surface, roll out the dough ⅛ inch thick. Transfer to a 10-inch tart pan. Trim the edge, prick the bottom and refrigerate.

5 ▲ Score the bottoms of the peaches. Drop the peaches, one at a time, into boiling water. Boil for 20 seconds, then dip in cold water. Peel off the skins using a sharp knife.

6 ▲ Grind the almonds finely with the flour in a food processor, blender, or nut grinder. With an electric mixer, cream the butter and ½ cup of the sugar until light and fluffy. Gradually beat in the egg and yolk. Stir in the almonds and vanilla or rum. Spread in the pastry shell.

7 ▲ Halve the peaches and remove the stones. Cut crosswise in thin slices and arrange on top of the almond cream like the spokes of a wheel; keep the slices of each peach half together. Fan out by pressing down gently at a slight angle.

8 ▲ Bake until the pastry begins to brown, 10–15 minutes. Lower the heat to 350°F and continue baking until the almond cream sets, about 15 minutes more. Ten minutes before the end of the cooking time, sprinkle with the remaining 2 tablespoons of sugar.

~ VARIATION ~

For a Nectarine and Apricot Tart with Almond Cream, replace the peaches with nectarines, prepared and arranged the same way. Peel and chop 3 fresh apricots. Fill the spaces between the fanned-out nectarines with 1 tablespoon of chopped apricots. Bake as above.

Apple-Cranberry Lattice Pie

SERVES 8

grated rind of 1 orange

3 tablespoons fresh orange juice

2 large, tart cooking apples

1 cup cranberries

½ cup raisins

¼ cup walnuts, chopped

1 cup plus tablespoon granulated sugar

½ cup dark brown sugar, firmly packed

1 tablespoon quick-cooking tapioca

FOR THE CRUST

2 cups flour

½ teaspoon salt

6 tablespoons cold butter, cut in pieces

4 tablespoons cold shortening, cut in pieces

¼–½ cup ice water

1 ▼ For the crust, sift the flour and salt into a bowl. Add the butter and shortening and rub with your fingertips until the mixture resembles coarse crumbs, or use a pastry blender. With a fork, stir in just enough water to bind the dough. Gather into 2 equal balls, wrap in wax paper, and refrigerate for at least 20 minutes.

2 ▲ Put the orange rind and juice into a mixing bowl. Peel and core the apples and grate them into the bowl. Stir in the cranberries, raisins, walnuts, 1 cup of the granulated sugar, brown sugar, and tapioca.

3 Place a baking sheet in the oven and preheat to 400°F.

4 On a lightly floured surface, roll out 1 ball of dough about ⅛ inch thick. Transfer to a 9-inch pie pan and trim the edge. Spoon the cranberry and apple mixture into the shell.

5 ▲ Roll out the remaining dough to a circle about 11 inches in diameter. With a serrated pastry wheel, cut the dough into 10 strips, ¾ inch wide. Place 5 strips horizontally across the top of the tart at 1-inch intervals. Weave in 5 vertical strips. Trim the edges. Sprinkle the top with the remaining 1 tablespoon sugar.

6 Bake for 20 minutes. Reduce the heat to 350°F and bake until the crust is golden and the filling is bubbling, about 15 minutes more.

Open Apple Pie

SERVES 8

3 pounds sweet-tart firm eating or
cooking apples

¼ cup sugar

2 teaspoons ground cinnamon

grated rind and juice of 1 lemon

2 tablespoons butter, diced

2–3 tablespoons honey

FOR THE CRUST

2 cups flour

½ teaspoon salt

½ cup (1 stick) cold butter, cut in
pieces

3 tablespoons cold shortening, cut in
pieces

5–6 tablespoons ice water

1 For the crust, sift the flour and salt
into a bowl. Add the butter and
shortening and cut in with a pastry
blender until the mixture resembles
coarse crumbs.

2 ▲ With a fork, stir in just enough
water to bind the dough. Gather into
a ball, wrap in wax paper, and
refrigerate for at least 20 minutes.

3 Place a baking sheet in the center
of the oven and preheat to 400°F.

4 ▼ Peel, core, and slice the apples.
Combine the sugar and cinnamon in a
bowl. Add the apples, lemon rind and
juice, and stir.

5 On a lightly floured surface, roll out
the dough to a circle about 12 inches
in diameter. Transfer to a 9-inch
diameter deep pie dish; leave the
dough hanging over the edge. Fill
with the apple slices.

6 ▲ Fold in the edges and crimp
loosely for a decorative border. Dot
the apples with diced butter.

7 Bake on the hot sheet until the
pastry is golden and the apples are
tender, about 45 minutes.

8 Melt the honey in a saucepan and
brush over the apples to glaze. Serve
warm or at room temperature.

Apple Pie

SERVES 8

2 pounds tart cooking apples

2 tablespoons flour

½ cup sugar

1½ tablespoons fresh lemon juice

½ teaspoon ground cinnamon

½ teaspoon ground allspice

¼ teaspoon ground ginger

¼ teaspoon grated nutmeg

¼ teaspoon salt

4 tablespoons butter, diced

FOR THE CRUST

2 cups flour

1 teaspoon salt

6 tablespoons cold butter, cut in pieces

4 tablespoons cold shortening, cut in pieces

¼–½ cup ice water

1 ▲ For the crust, sift the flour and salt into a bowl.

2 Add the butter and shortening and cut in with a pastry blender or rub between your fingertips until the mixture resembles coarse crumbs. With a fork, stir in just enough water to bind the dough.

3 ▲ Gather into 2 balls, wrap in wax paper and refrigerate for 20 minutes.

4 ▲ On a lightly floured surface, roll out 1 dough ball ⅛ inch thick. Transfer to a 9-inch pie pan and trim the edge. Place a baking sheet in the center of the oven and preheat to 425°F.

5 ▲ Peel, core, and slice the apples into a bowl. Toss with the flour, sugar, lemon juice, spices, and salt. Spoon into pie shell; dot with butter.

6 ▲ Roll out the remaining dough. Place on top of the pie and trim to leave a ¾-inch overhang. Fold the overhang under the bottom dough and press to seal. Crimp the edge.

7 ▲ Roll out the scraps and cut out leaf shapes and roll balls. Arrange on top of the pie. Cut steam vents.

8 Bake for 10 minutes. Reduce the heat to 350°F and bake until golden, 40–45 minutes more. If the pie browns too quickly, protect with foil.

~ COOK'S TIP ~

Select apples that are firm and tart, such as Jonathan, Greening, Granny Smith or Winesap. Macintosh and Delicious soften too much during cooking.

Pear-Apple Crumb Pie

SERVES 8

3 firm pears

4 tart cooking apples

¾ cup sugar

2 tablespoons cornstarch

⅛ teaspoon salt

grated rind of 1 lemon

2 tablespoons fresh lemon juice

½ cup raisins

¾ cup flour

1 teaspoon ground cinnamon

6 tablespoons cold butter, cut in pieces

FOR THE CRUST

1 cup flour

½ teaspoon salt

⅓ cup cold shortening, cut in pieces

2 tablespoons ice water

1 For the crust, combine the flour and salt in a bowl. Add the shortening and cut in with a pastry blender until the mixture resembles coarse crumbs. With a fork, stir in just enough water to bind the dough. Gather into a ball and transfer to a lightly floured surface. Roll out about ⅛ inch thick.

2 ▲ Transfer to a shallow 9-inch pie pan and trim to leave a ½-inch overhang. Fold the overhang under for a double thickness. Flute the edge with your fingers. Refrigerate.

3 Place a baking sheet in the oven and preheat to 450°F.

4 ▲ Peel and core the pears. Slice them into a bowl. Peel, core, and slice the apples. Add to the pears. Stir in ⅓ cup of the sugar, the cornstarch, salt, and lemon rind. Add the lemon juice and raisins and stir to blend.

5 For the crumb topping, combine the remaining sugar, flour, cinnamon, and butter in a bowl. Blend with your fingertips until the mixture resembles coarse crumbs. Set aside.

6 ▲ Spoon the fruit filling into the pie shell. Sprinkle the crumbs lightly and evenly over the top.

7 Bake for 10 minutes, then reduce the heat to 350°F. Cover the top of the pie loosely with a sheet of foil and continue baking until browned, 35–40 minutes more.

Chocolate Pear Tart

SERVES 8

4 1-ounce squares semisweet chocolate, grated
3 large firm, ripe pears
1 egg
1 egg yolk
½ cup light cream
½ teaspoon vanilla extract
3 tablespoons sugar
FOR THE CRUST
1 cup flour
⅛ teaspoon salt
2 tablespoons sugar
½ cup (1 stick) cold unsalted butter, cut into pieces
1 egg yolk
1 tablespoon fresh lemon juice

1 For the crust, sift the flour and salt into a bowl. Add the sugar and butter. Cut in with a pastry blender until the mixture resembles coarse crumbs. With a fork, stir in the egg yolk and lemon juice until the mixture forms a dough. Gather into a ball, wrap in wax paper, and refrigerate for at least 20 minutes.

2 Place a baking sheet in the oven and preheat to 400°F.

3 On a lightly floured surface, roll out the dough ⅛ inch thick and trim the edge. Transfer to a 10-inch tart pan.

4 ▲ Sprinkle the bottom of the tart shell with the grated chocolate.

5 ▲ Peel, halve, and core the pears. Cut in thin slices crosswise, then fan them out slightly.

6 Transfer the pear halves to the tart with the help of a metal spatula and arrange on top of the chocolate like the spokes of a wheel.

7 ▼ Whisk together the egg and egg yolk, cream, and vanilla. Ladle over the pears, then sprinkle with sugar.

8 Bake for 10 minutes. Reduce the heat to 350°F and cook until the custard is set and the pears begin to caramelize, about 20 minutes more. Serve at room temperature.

Caramelized Upside-Down Pear Pie

SERVES 8

5–6 firm, ripe pears

¾ cup sugar

½ cup (1 stick) unsalted butter

whipped cream, for serving

FOR THE CRUST

¾ cup all-purpose flour

¼ cup cake flour

¼ teaspoon salt

9 tablespoons cold butter, cut in pieces

3 tablespoons cold shortening, cut in pieces

¼ cup ice water

1 ▲ For the crust, combine the flours and salt in a bowl. Add the butter and shortening and cut in with a pastry blender until the mixture resembles coarse crumbs. With a fork, stir in just enough water to bind the dough. Gather into a ball, wrap in wax paper, and refrigerate for at least 20 minutes.

2 Preheat the oven to 400°F.

~ **VARIATION** ~

For Caramelized Upside-Down Apple Pie, replace the pears with 8–9 firm, tart apples. There may seem to be too many apples, but they shrink slightly as they cook.

3 ▲ Quarter, peel and core the pears. Place in a bowl and toss with a few tablespoons of the sugar.

4 ▲ In a 10½-inch ovenproof skillet, melt the butter over moderately high heat. Add the remaining sugar. When it starts to color, arrange the pears evenly around the edge and in the center.

5 ▲ Continue cooking, uncovered, until caramelized, about 20 minutes.

6 ▲ Let the fruit cool. Roll out a circle of dough slightly larger than the diameter of the skillet. Place the dough on top of the pears, tucking in around the edges.

7 Bake for 15 minutes, then reduce the heat to 350°F. Bake until golden, about 15 minutes more.

8 ▲ Let the pie cool in the pan for 3 minutes. To unmold, run a knife around the edge, then, using oven gloves, place a plate bottom-side up over the skillet and quickly invert the two together.

9 If any pears stick to the skillet, remove gently with a metal spatula and replace them carefully on the pie. Serve warm, with the whipped cream passed separately.

Key Lime Pie

SERVES 8

3 large egg yolks

1 14-ounce can sweetened condensed milk

1 tablespoon grated Key lime rind

½ cup fresh Key lime juice

green food coloring (optional)

½ cup whipping cream

FOR THE CRUST

1¼ cups graham cracker crumbs

5 tablespoons butter or margarine, melted

1 Preheat the oven to 350°F.

2 ▲ For the crust, place the graham cracker crumbs in a bowl and add the butter or margarine. Mix to combine.

~ **VARIATION** ~

If Key limes are not available, use regular limes.

3 Press the crumbs evenly over the bottom and sides of a 9-inch pie pan. Bake for 8 minutes. Let cool.

4 ▲ Beat the yolks until thick. Beat in the milk, lime rind and juice, and coloring, if using. Pour into the prebaked pie shell and refrigerate until set, about 4 hours. To serve, whip the cream. Pipe a lattice pattern on top, or spoon dollops around the edge.

Fruit Tartlets

MAKES 8

¾ cup red currant or grape jelly

1 tablespoon fresh lemon juice

¾ cup whipping cream

1½ pounds fresh fruit, such as strawberries, raspberries, kiwi fruit, peaches, grapes, or blueberries, peeled and sliced as necessary

FOR THE CRUST

⅔ cup (10⅔ tablespoons) cold butter, cut in pieces

⅓ cup dark brown sugar, firmly packed

3 tablespoons unsweetened cocoa powder

1½ cups flour

1 egg white

1 For the crust, combine the butter, brown sugar, and cocoa over low heat. When the butter is melted, remove from the heat and sift over the flour. Stir, then add just enough egg white to bind the mixture. Gather into a ball, wrap in wax paper, and refrigerate for at least 30 minutes.

2 ▲ Grease 8 3-inch tartlet pans. Roll out the dough between two sheets of wax paper. Stamp out 8 4-inch rounds with a fluted cutter.

3 Line the tartlet pans with dough. Prick the bottoms. Refrigerate for 15 minutes. Preheat the oven to 350°F.

4 Bake until firm, 20–25 minutes. Cool, then remove from the pans.

5 ▲ Melt the jelly with the lemon juice. Brush a thin layer in the bottom of the tartlets. Whip the cream and spread a thin layer in the tartlet shells. Arrange the fruit on top. Brush with the glaze and serve.

Key Lime Pie (top), Fruit Tartlets

Chocolate Lemon Tart

SERVES 8–10

1¼ cups granulated sugar

6 eggs

grated rind of 2 lemons

⅔ cup fresh lemon juice

⅔ cup whipping cream

chocolate curls, for decorating

FOR THE CRUST

1¼ cups flour

2 tablespoons unsweetened cocoa powder

4 tablespoons confectioners' sugar

½ teaspoon salt

½ cup (1 stick) butter or margarine

1 tablespoon water

1 ▲ Grease a 10-inch tart pan.

2 For the crust, sift the flour, cocoa powder, confectioners' sugar, and salt into a bowl. Set aside.

3 ▲ Melt the butter and water over low heat. Pour over the flour mixture and stir with a wooden spoon until the dough is smooth and the flour has absorbed all the liquid.

4 Press the dough evenly over the base and sides of the prepared tart pan. Refrigerate the tart shell while preparing the filling.

5 Place a baking sheet in the center of the oven and preheat to 375°F.

6 ▲ Whisk the sugar and eggs until the sugar is dissolved. Add the lemon rind and juice and mix well. Add the cream. Taste the mixture and add more lemon juice or sugar if needed. It should taste tart but also sweet.

7 Pour the filling into the tart shell and bake on the hot sheet until the filling is set, 20–25 minutes. Cool on a rack. When cool, sprinkle with the chocolate curls.

Lemon Almond Tart

SERVES 8

¾ cup blanched almonds

½ cup sugar

2 eggs

grated rind and juice of 1½ lemons

½ cup (1 stick) butter, melted

strips of lemon rind, for decorating

FOR THE CRUST

1¼ cups flour

1 tablespoon sugar

½ teaspoon salt

½ teaspoon baking powder

6 tablespoons cold unsalted butter, cut in pieces

3–4 tablespoons whipping cream

1 For the crust, sift the flour, sugar, salt, and baking powder into a bowl. Add the butter and cut in with a pastry blender until the mixture resembles coarse crumbs.

2 ▲ With a fork, stir in just enough cream to bind the dough.

3 Gather into a ball and transfer to a lightly floured surface. Roll out the dough about ⅛ inch thick and transfer to a 9-inch tart pan. Trim the edge. Prick the base all over with a fork and refrigerate for at least 20 minutes.

4 Set a baking sheet in the center of the oven and preheat to 400°F.

5 Line the tart shell with crumpled wax paper and fill with pie weights. Bake for 12 minutes. Remove the paper and weights and continue baking until golden, 6–8 minutes more. Reduce the oven temperature to 350°F.

6 ▲ Grind the almonds finely with 1 tablespoon of the sugar in a food processor, blender, or nut grinder.

7 ▲ Set a mixing bowl over a pan of hot water. Add the eggs and the remaining sugar, and beat with an electric mixer until the mixture is thick enough to leave a ribbon trail when the beaters are lifted.

8 Stir in the lemon rind and juice, butter, and ground almonds.

9 Pour into the prebaked shell. Bake until the filling is golden and set, about 35 minutes. Decorate with lemon rind.

Lemon Meringue Pie

SERVES 8

grated rind and juice of 1 large lemon

1 cup plus 1 tablespoon cold water

½ cup plus 6 tablespoons sugar

2 tablespoons butter

3 tablespoons cornstarch

3 eggs, separated

⅛ teaspoon salt

⅛ teaspoon cream of tartar

FOR THE CRUST

1 cup flour

½ teaspoon salt

⅓ cup (5⅓ tablespoons) cold shortening, cut in pieces

2 tablespoons ice water

1 For the crust, sift the flour and salt into a bowl. Add the shortening and cut in with a pastry blender until the mixture resembles coarse crumbs. With a fork, stir in just enough water to bind the dough. Gather the dough into a ball.

2 ▲ On a lightly floured surface, roll out the dough about ⅛ inch thick. Transfer to a 9-inch pie pan and trim the edge to leave a ½-inch overhang.

3 ▲ Fold the overhang under and crimp the edge. Refrigerate the pie shell for at least 20 minutes.

4 Preheat the oven to 400°F.

5 ▲ Prick the dough all over with a fork. Line with crumpled wax paper and fill with pie weights. Bake for 12 minutes. Remove the paper and weights and continue baking until golden, 6–8 minutes more.

6 In a saucepan, combine the lemon rind and juice, 1 cup of the water, ½ cup of the sugar, and butter. Bring the mixture to a boil.

7 Meanwhile, in a mixing bowl, dissolve the cornstarch in the remaining water. Add the egg yolks.

> ~ **VARIATION** ~
>
> For Lime Meringue Pie, substitute the grated rind and juice of 2 medium-sized limes for the lemon.

8 ▲ Add the egg yolks to the lemon mixture and return to a boil, whisking continuously until the mixture thickens, about 5 minutes.

9 Cover the surface with wax paper to prevent a skin forming and let cool.

10 ▲ For the meringue, using an electric mixer beat the egg whites with the salt and cream of tartar until they hold stiff peaks. Add the remaining sugar and beat until glossy.

11 ▲ Spoon the lemon mixture into the pie shell and spread level. Spoon the meringue on top, smoothing it up to the edge of the crust to seal. Bake until golden, 12–15 minutes.

Orange Tart

SERVES 8

1 cup sugar

1 cup fresh orange juice, strained

2 large navel oranges

¾ cup blanched almonds

4 tablespoons butter

1 egg

1 tablespoon flour

3 tablespoons apricot jam

FOR THE CRUST

1½ cups flour

½ teaspoon salt

4 tablespoons cold butter, cut in pieces

3 tablespoons cold margarine, cut in pieces

3–4 tablespoons ice water

1 For the crust, sift the flour and salt into a bowl. Add the butter and margarine and cut in with a pastry blender until the mixture resembles coarse crumbs. Stir in just enough water to bind the dough. Gather into a ball, wrap in wax paper, and refrigerate for at least 20 minutes.

2 On a lightly floured surface, roll out the dough ¼ inch thick and transfer to an 8-inch tart pan. Trim off the overhang. Refrigerate until needed.

3 In a saucepan, combine ¾ cup of the sugar and the orange juice and boil until thick and syrupy, about 10 minutes.

4 ▲ Cut the oranges into ¼-inch slices. Do not peel. Add to the syrup. Simmer gently for 10 minutes, or until glazed. Transfer to a rack to dry. When cool, cut in half. Reserve the syrup. Place a baking sheet in the oven and heat to 400°F.

5 Grind the almonds finely in a food processor, blender or nut grinder. With an electric mixer, cream the butter and remaining sugar until light and fluffy. Beat in the egg and 2 tablespoons of the orange syrup. Stir in the almonds and flour.

6 Melt the jam over low heat, then brush in the tart shell. Pour in the almond mixture. Bake until set, about 20 minutes. Let cool.

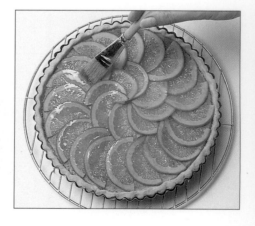

7 ▲ Arrange overlapping orange slices on top. Boil the remaining syrup until thick. Brush on top to glaze.

Pumpkin Pie

SERVES 8

2 cups cooked or canned pumpkin

1 cup whipping cream

2 eggs

½ cup dark brown sugar, firmly packed

4 tablespoons light corn syrup

1½ teaspoons ground cinnamon

1 teaspoon ground ginger

¼ teaspoon ground cloves

½ teaspoon salt

FOR THE CRUST

1½ cup flour

½ teaspoon salt

6 tablespoons cold butter, cut in pieces

3 tablespoons cold shortening, cut in pieces

3–4 tablespoons ice water

1 For the crust, sift the flour and salt into a bowl. Cut in the butter and shortening with a pastry blender until the mixture resembles coarse crumbs. Stir in just enough water to bind. Gather into a ball, wrap in wax paper and refrigerate for 20 minutes.

2 Roll out the dough ⅛ inch thick. Transfer to a 9-inch pie pan. Trim off the overhang. Roll out the trimmings and cut out leaf shapes. Moisten the edges with a brush dipped in water.

3 ▲ Arrange the dough leaves around the edge. Refrigerate for 20 minutes. Preheat the oven to 400°F.

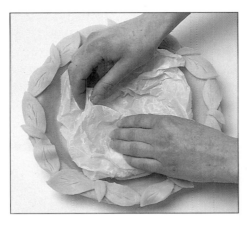

4 ▲ Prick the bottom with a fork and line with crumpled wax paper. Fill with pie weights and bake for 12 minutes. Remove paper and weights and bake until golden, 6–8 minutes more. Reduce the heat to 375°F.

5 ▼ Beat together the pumpkin, cream, eggs, sugar, corn syrup, spices, and salt. Pour into the shell and bake until set, about 40 minutes.

Maple Walnut Pie

SERVES 8

3 eggs

⅛ teaspoon salt

¼ cup granulated sugar

4 tablespoons butter or margarine, melted

1 cup pure maple syrup

1 cup walnuts, chopped

whipped cream, for decorating

FOR THE CRUST

½ cup all-purpose flour

½ cup whole-wheat flour

⅛ teaspoon salt

4 tablespoons cold butter, cut in pieces

3 tablespoons cold shortening, cut in pieces

1 egg yolk

2–3 tablespoons ice water

1 ▼ For the crust, mix the flours and salt in a bowl. Add the butter and shortening and cut in with a pastry blender until the mixture resembles coarse crumbs. With a fork, stir in the egg yolk and just enough water to bind the dough.

2 Gather into a ball, wrap in wax paper, and refrigerate for 20 minutes.

3 Preheat the oven to 425°F.

4 On a lightly floured surface, roll out the dough about ⅛ inch thick and transfer to a 9-inch pie pan. Trim the edge. To decorate, roll out the trimmings. With a small heart-shaped cutter, stamp out enough hearts to go around the rim of the pie. Brush the edge with water, then arrange the dough hearts all around.

5 ▲ Prick the bottom with a fork. Line with crumpled wax paper and fill with pie weights. Bake 10 minutes. Remove the paper and weights and continue baking until golden brown, 3–6 minutes more.

6 In a bowl, whisk the eggs, salt, and sugar together. Stir in the butter or margarine and maple syrup.

7 ▲ Set the pie shell on a baking sheet. Pour in the filling, then sprinkle the nuts over the top.

8 Bake until just set, about 35 minutes. Cool on a rack. Decorate with whipped cream, if wished.

Pecan Tart

SERVES 8

3 eggs

⅛ teaspoon of salt

1 cup dark brown sugar, firmly packed

½ cup dark corn syrup

2 tablespoons fresh lemon juice

6 tablespoons butter, melted

1½ cups pecans, chopped

½ cup pecan halves

FOR THE CRUST

1¼ cups flour

1 tablespoon granulated sugar

1 teaspoon baking powder

½ teaspoon salt

6 tablespoons cold unsalted butter, cut in pieces

1 egg yolk

3–4 tablespoons whipping cream

1 For the crust, sift the flour, sugar, baking powder, and salt into a bowl. Add the butter and cut in with a pastry blender until the mixture resembles coarse crumbs.

2 ▼ In a bowl, beat together the egg yolk and cream until blended.

~ COOK'S TIP ~

Serve this tart warm, accompanied by ice cream or whipped cream, if wished.

3 ▲ Pour the cream mixture into the flour mixture and stir with a fork.

4 Gather the dough into a ball. On a lightly floured surface, roll out ⅛ inch thick and transfer to a 9-inch tart pan. Trim the overhang and flute the edge with your fingers. Refrigerate for at least 20 minutes.

5 Set a baking sheet in the middle of the oven and preheat to 400°F.

6 In a bowl, lightly whisk the eggs and salt. Add the sugar, corn syrup, lemon juice, and butter. Mix well and stir in the chopped nuts.

7 ▲ Pour into the pastry shell and arrange the pecan halves in concentric circles on top.

8 Bake for 10 minutes. Reduce the heat to 325°F; continue baking 25 minutes more.

Mince Pies

MAKES 36

1 cup blanched almonds, finely chopped

1 cup dried apricots, finely chopped

1 cup raisins

1 cup currants

1 cup candied cherries, chopped

1 cup candied citrus peel, chopped

1 cup finely chopped beef suet

grated rind and juice of 2 lemons

grated rind and juice of 1 orange

1 cup dark brown sugar, firmly packed

4 tart cooking apples, peeled, cored and chopped

2 teaspoons ground cinnamon

1 teaspoon grated nutmeg

½ teaspoon ground cloves

1 cup brandy

8 ounces cream cheese

2 tablespoons granulated sugar

confectioners' sugar, for dusting

FOR THE CRUST

3 cups flour

1¼ cups confectioners' sugar

1½ cups (3 sticks) cold butter, cut in pieces

grated rind and juice of 1 orange

milk, for glazing

1 Mix the nuts, dried and candied fruit, suet, citrus rind and juice, brown sugar, apples, and spices in a bowl.

2 ▲ Stir in the brandy. Cover and leave in a cool place for 2 days.

3 For the crust, sift the flour and confectioners' sugar into a bowl. Cut in the butter until the mixture resembles coarse crumbs.

4 ▲ Add the orange rind. Stir in just enough orange juice to bind. Gather into a ball, wrap in wax paper, and refrigerate for at least 20 minutes.

5 Preheat the oven to 425°F. Grease 2–3 muffin pans. Beat together the cream cheese and granulated sugar.

6 ▲ Roll out the dough ¼ inch thick. With a fluted pastry cutter, stamp out 36 3-inch rounds.

~ **COOK'S TIP** ~

The mincemeat mixture may be packed into sterilized jars and sealed. It will keep refrigerated for several months. Add a few tablespoonfuls to give apple pies a lift, or make small mincemeat-filled parcels using phyllo pastry.

7 ▲ Transfer the rounds to the muffin pans. Fill halfway with mincemeat. Top with a teaspoonful of the cream cheese mixture.

8 ▲ Roll out the pastry trimmings and stamp out 36 2-inch rounds with a fluted cutter. Brush the edges of the pies with milk, then set the rounds on top. Cut a small steam vent in the top of each pie.

9 ▲ Brush lightly with milk. Bake until golden, 15–20 minutes. Let cool for 10 minutes before unmolding. Dust with confectioners' sugar.

Shoofly Pie

SERVES 8

1 cup flour
½ cup dark brown sugar, firmly packed
¼ teaspoon each salt, ground ginger, cinnamon, mace, and grated nutmeg
6 tablespoons cold butter, cut in pieces
2 eggs
½ cup molasses
½ cup boiling water
½ teaspoon baking soda
FOR THE CRUST
4 ounces cream cheese, at room temperature, cut in pieces
½ cup (1 stick) cold butter, at room temperature, cut in pieces
1 cup flour

1 For the crust, put the cream cheese and butter in a mixing bowl. Sift over the flour.

2 ▲ Cut in with a pastry blender until the dough just holds together. Wrap in wax paper and refrigerate for at least 30 minutes.

3 Set a baking sheet in the center of the oven and preheat to 375°F.

4 In a bowl, mix together the flour, sugar, salt, spices, and cold butter pieces. Blend with your fingertips until the mixture resembles coarse crumbs. Set aside.

5 On a lightly floured surface, roll out the dough ⅛ inch thick and transfer to a 9-inch pie pan. Trim the overhang and flute the edges.

6 ▲ Spoon one-third of the crumbs into the pie shell.

7 ▲ To complete the filling, whisk the eggs with the molasses in a large bowl.

8 Measure the boiling water into a small bowl and stir in the soda; it will foam. Pour immediately into the egg mixture and whisk to blend. Pour carefully into the pie shell and sprinkle the remaining crumbs over the top in an even layer.

9 Bake on the hot sheet until browned, about 35 minutes. Let cool, then serve at room temperature.

Treacle Tart

SERVES 4–6

¾ cup dark corn syrup
1½ cups fresh white bread crumbs
grated rind of 1 lemon
2 tablespoons fresh lemon juice
FOR THE CRUST
1¼ cups flour
½ teaspoon salt
6 tablespoons cold butter, cut in pieces
3 tablespoons cold margarine, cut in pieces
3–4 tablespoons ice water

1 For the crust, combine the flour and salt in a bowl. Add the butter and margarine and cut in with a pastry blender until the mixture resembles coarse crumbs.

2 ▲ With a fork, stir in just enough water to bind the dough. Gather into a ball, wrap in wax paper, and refrigerate for at least 20 minutes.

3 On a lightly floured surface, roll out the dough ⅛ inch thick. Transfer to an 8-inch tart pan and trim off the overhang. Refrigerate for at least 20 minutes. Reserve the trimmings for the lattice top.

4 Place a baking sheet above the center of the oven and heat to 400°F.

5 In a saucepan, warm the corn syrup until thin and runny.

6 ▲ Remove from the heat and stir in the bread crumbs and lemon rind. Let sit for 10 minutes so the bread can absorb the syrup. Add more bread crumbs if the mixture is thin. Stir in the lemon juice and spread evenly in the pastry shell.

7 Roll out the pastry trimmings and cut into 10–12 thin strips.

8 ▼ Lay half the strips on the filling, then arrange the remaining strips to form a lattice pattern.

9 Place on the hot sheet and bake for 10 minutes. Lower the heat to 375°F. Bake until golden, about 15 minutes more. Serve warm or cold.

Chess Pie

SERVES 8

2 eggs
3 tablespoons whipping cream
½ cup dark brown sugar, firmly packed
2 tablespoons granulated sugar
2 tablespoons flour
1 tablespoon bourbon or whisky
3 tablespoons butter, melted
½ cup walnuts, chopped
¾ cup pitted dates
whipped cream, for serving
FOR THE CRUST
6 tablespoons cold butter
3 tablespoons cold shortening
1½ cups flour
½ teaspoon salt
3–4 tablespoons ice water

1 ▲ For the crust, cut the butter and shortening in small pieces.

2 Sift the flour and salt into a bowl. With a pastry blender, cut in the butter and margarine until the mixture resembles coarse crumbs. Stir in just enough water to bind. Gather into a ball, wrap in wax paper, and refrigerate for at least 20 minutes.

3 Place a baking sheet in the center of the oven and preheat to 375°F.

4 Roll out the dough ⅛ inch thick. Transfer to a 9-inch pie pan and trim the edge. Roll out the trimmings, cut thin strips and braid them. Brush the edge of the pie with water and place the dough braid around the edge.

5 ▲ In a mixing bowl, whisk together the eggs and cream.

6 Add both sugars and beat until well combined. Sift over 1 tablespoon of the flour and stir in. Add the bourbon or whisky, the melted butter, and the walnuts. Stir to combine.

7 ▲ Mix the dates with the remaining tablespoon of flour and stir into the walnut mixture.

8 Pour into the pie shell and bake until the pastry is golden and the filling puffed up, about 35 minutes. Serve at room temperature, with whipped cream if desired.

Coconut Cream Pie

SERVES 8

2½ cups flaked sweetened coconut

⅔ cup sugar

4 tablespoons cornstarch

⅛ teaspoon salt

2½ cups milk

¼ cup whipping cream

2 egg yolks

2 tablespoons unsalted butter

2 teaspoons vanilla extract

FOR THE CRUST

1 cup flour

¼ teaspoon salt

3 tablespoons cold butter, cut in pieces

2 tablespoons cold shortening

2–3 tablespoons ice water

1 For the crust, sift the flour and salt into a bowl. Add the butter and shortening and cut in with a pastry blender until the mixture resembles coarse crumbs.

2 ▲ With a fork, stir in just enough water to bind the dough. Gather into a ball, wrap in wax paper, and refrigerate for at least 20 minutes.

3 Preheat the oven to 425°F. Roll out the dough ⅛ inch thick. Transfer to a 9-inch pie pan. Trim and flute the edges. Prick the bottom. Line with crumpled wax paper and fill with pie weights. Bake for 10–12 minutes. Remove the paper and weights, reduce the heat to 350°F and bake until brown, 10–15 minutes more.

4 ▲ Spread 1 cup of the coconut on a baking sheet and toast in the oven until golden, 6–8 minutes, stirring often. Set aside for decorating.

5 Put the sugar, cornstarch, and salt in a saucepan. In a bowl, whisk the milk, cream, and egg yolks. Add the egg mixture to the saucepan.

6 ▼ Cook over low heat, stirring constantly, until the mixture comes to a boil. Boil for 1 minute, then remove from the heat. Add the butter, vanilla, and remaining coconut.

7 Pour into the prebaked pie shell. When cool, sprinkle toasted coconut in a ring in the center.

Black Bottom Pie

SERVES 8

2 teaspoons unflavored gelatin

3 tablespoons cold water

2 eggs, separated

1 cup sugar

2 tablespoons cornstarch

½ teaspoon salt

2 cups milk

2 1-ounce squares unsweetened
    chocolate, finely chopped

3 tablespoons rum

¼ teaspoon cream of tartar

chocolate curls, for decorating

FOR THE CRUST

1½ cups gingersnap cookie crumbs

⅓ cup (5⅓ tablespoons) butter, melted

1 Preheat the oven to 350°F.

2 For the crust, mix the cookie crumbs and melted butter.

3 ▲ Press the mixture evenly over the bottom and sides of a 9-inch pie pan. Bake for 6 minutes. Let cool.

4 Sprinkle the gelatin over the water and let stand to soften.

5 Beat the egg yolks in a large mixing bowl and set aside.

6 In a saucepan, combine half the sugar, the cornstarch, and salt. Gradually stir in the milk. Boil for 1 minute, stirring constantly.

7 ▲ Whisk the hot milk mixture into the yolks, then pour all back into the saucepan and return to a boil, whisking. Cook for 1 minute, still whisking. Remove from the heat.

8 ▲ Measure out 1 cup of the hot custard mixture and pour into a bowl. Add the chopped chocolate to the custard mixture, and stir until melted. Stir in half the rum and pour into the pie crust.

9 ▲ Whisk the softened gelatin into the plain custard until it has dissolved, then stir in the remaining rum. Set the pan in cold water until it reaches room temperature.

10 ▲ With an electric mixer, beat the egg whites and cream of tartar until they hold stiff peaks. Beat in half the remaining sugar until glossy, then fold in the rest of the sugar.

11 ▲ Fold the custard into the egg whites, then spoon over the chocolate mixture in the pie shell. Refrigerate until set, about 2 hours.

12 Decorate the top with chocolate curls. Keep the pie refrigerated until ready to serve.

~ COOK'S TIP ~

To make chocolate curls, melt 8 ounces semisweet chocolate over hot water, stir in 1 tablespoon of neutral vegetable oil, and mold in a small foil-lined loaf pan. For large curls, soften the bar between your hands and carve off curls from the wide side with a vegetable peeler; for small curls, grate from the narrow side using a box grater.

Velvet Mocha Cream Pie

SERVES 8

2 teaspoons instant espresso coffee

2 tablespoons hot water

1½ cups whipping cream

6 1-ounce squares semisweet chocolate

1 1-ounce square unsweetened chocolate

½ cup whipped cream, for decorating

chocolate-covered coffee beans, for decorating

FOR THE CRUST

1½ cups chocolate wafer crumbs

2 tablespoons sugar

⅓ cup (5⅓ tablespoons) butter, melted

1 ▲ For the crust, mix the chocolate wafer crumbs and sugar together, then stir in the melted butter.

2 Press the crumbs evenly over the bottom and sides of a 9-inch pie pan. Refrigerate until firm.

3 In a bowl, dissolve the coffee in the water and set aside.

4 Melt both the chocolates in the top of a double boiler, or in a heatproof bowl set over a pan of hot water. Remove from the heat when nearly melted and stir to continue melting. Set the bottom of the pan in cool water to reduce the temperature. Be careful not to splash any water on the chocolate or it will become grainy.

5 Pour the cream into a mixing bowl. Set the bowl in hot water to warm the cream, bringing it closer to the temperature of the chocolate.

6 ▲ With an electric mixer, whip the cream until it is lightly fluffy. Add the dissolved coffee and whip until the cream just holds its shape.

7 ▲ When the chocolate is at room temperature, fold it gently into the cream with a large metal spoon.

8 Pour into the chilled pastry case and refrigerate until firm. To serve, pipe a ring of whipped cream rosettes around the edge, then place a chocolate-covered coffee bean in the center of each rosette.

Brandy Alexander Tart

SERVES 8

½ cup cold water
1 tablespoon unflavored gelatin
½ cup sugar
3 eggs, separated
4 tablespoons brandy or cognac
4 tablespoons crème de cacao
⅛ teaspoon of salt
1¼ cups whipping cream
chocolate curls, for decorating
FOR THE CRUST
1¼ cups graham cracker crumbs
5 tablespoons butter, melted
1 tablespoon sugar

1 Preheat the oven to 375°F.

2 For the crust, mix the graham cracker crumbs with the butter and sugar in a bowl.

3 ▲ Press the crumbs evenly into the bottom and sides of a 9-inch tart pan. Bake until just brown, about 10 minutes. Cool on a rack.

4 Place the water in the top of a double boiler set over hot water. Sprinkle over the gelatin and let stand for 5 minutes to soften. Add half the sugar and the egg yolks. Whisk continually over a very low heat until the gelatin dissolves and the mixture thickens slightly. Do not allow the mixture to boil.

5 ▲ Remove from the heat and stir in the brandy and crème de cacao.

6 Set the pan over ice water and stir occasionally until it cools and thickens; it should not set firmly.

7 With an electric mixer, beat the egg whites and salt until they hold stiff peaks. Beat in the remaining sugar. Spoon a large dollop of whites into the yolk mixture and fold in to lighten.

8 ▼ Pour the egg yolk mixture over the remaining whites and fold together gently.

9 Whip the cream until soft peaks form, then gently fold into the filling. Spoon into the prebaked crust and chill until set, 3–4 hours. Decorate with chocolate curls before serving.

Nesselrode Pie

SERVES 10

1 tablespoon rum

¼ cup candied fruit, chopped

2 cups milk

4 teaspoons unflavored gelatin

½ cup sugar

½ teaspoon salt

3 eggs, separated

1 cup whipping cream

chocolate curls, for decorating

FOR THE CRUST

1¼ cups graham cracker crumbs

5 tablespoons butter, melted

1 tablespoon sugar

1 For the crust, mix the graham cracker crumbs, butter, and sugar. Press evenly and firmly over the bottom and sides of a 9-inch pie pan. Refrigerate until firm.

2 ▲ In a bowl, stir together the rum and candied fruit. Set aside.

3 Pour ½ cup of the milk into a small bowl. Sprinkle over the gelatin and let stand 5 minutes to soften.

4 ▲ In the top of a double boiler, combine ¼ cup of the sugar, the remaining milk, and salt. Stir in the gelatin mixture. Cook over hot water, stirring, until gelatin dissolves.

5 Whisk in the egg yolks and cook, stirring, until thick enough to coat a spoon. Do not boil. Pour the custard over the candied fruit mixture. Set in a bowl of ice water to cool.

6 Whip the cream lightly. Set aside.

7 With an electric mixer, beat the egg whites until they hold soft peaks. Add the remaining sugar and beat just enough to blend. Fold in a large dollop of the egg whites into the cooled gelatin mixture. Pour into the remaining egg whites and carefully fold together. Fold in the cream.

8 ▲ Pour into the pie shell and chill until firm. Decorate the top with chocolate curls.

Chocolate Chiffon Pie

SERVES 8

6 1-ounce squares semisweet chocolate

1 1-ounce square unsweetened chocolate

1 cup milk

1 tablespoon unflavored gelatin

⅔ cup sugar

2 extra-large eggs, separated

1 teaspoon vanilla extract

1½ cup whipping cream

⅛ teaspoon salt

whipped cream and chocolate curls, for decorating

FOR THE CRUST

1½ cups graham cracker crumbs

6 tablespoons butter, melted

1 Place a baking sheet in the oven and preheat to 350°F.

2 For the crust, mix the graham cracker crumbs and butter in a bowl. Press the crumbs evenly over the bottom and sides of a 9-inch pie pan. Bake for 8 minutes. Let cool.

3 Chop the chocolate, then grind in a food processor or blender. Set aside.

4 Place the milk in the top of a double boiler. Sprinkle over the gelatin. Let stand 5 minutes to soften.

5 ▲ Set the top of the double boiler over hot water. Add ⅓ cup of the sugar, the chocolate, and egg yolks. Stir until dissolved. Add the vanilla.

6 ▲ Set the top of the double boiler in a bowl of ice and stir until the mixture reaches room temperature. Remove from the ice and set aside.

7 Whip the cream lightly. Set aside. With an electric mixer, beat the egg whites and salt until they hold soft peaks. Add the remaining sugar and beat only enough to blend.

8 Fold a dollop of egg whites into the chocolate mixture, then pour back into the whites and fold in.

9 ▲ Fold in the whipped cream and pour into the pastry shell. Put in the freezer until just set, about 5 minutes. If the center sinks, fill with any remaining mixture. Refrigerate for 3–4 hours. Decorate with whipped cream and chocolate curls. Serve cold.

Chocolate Cheesecake Pie

SERVES 8

12 ounces cream cheese

4 tablespoons whipping cream

1 cup sugar

½ cup unsweetened cocoa powder

½ teaspoon ground cinnamon

3 eggs

whipped cream, for decorating

chocolate curls, for decorating

FOR THE CRUST

1 cup graham cracker crumbs

½ cup crushed amaretti cookies (if unavailable, use all graham cracker crumbs for a total of 1½ cups)

6 tablespoons butter, melted

1 Place a baking sheet in the oven and preheat to 350°F.

2 For the crust, mix the crumbs and butter in a bowl.

3 ▲ With a spoon, press the crumbs evenly over the bottom and sides of a 9-inch pie pan. Bake for 8 minutes. Let cool. Keep the oven on.

4 With an electric mixer, beat the cheese and cream together until smooth. Beat in the sugar, cocoa, and cinnamon until blended.

5 ▼ Add the eggs, 1 at a time, beating just enough to blend.

6 Pour into the pie shell and bake on the hot sheet for 25–30 minutes. The filling will sink down as it cools. Decorate with whipped cream and chocolate curls.

Frozen Strawberry Pie

SERVES 8

8 ounces cream cheese

1 cup sour cream

2 10-ounce packages frozen sliced strawberries, thawed

FOR THE CRUST

1¼ cup graham cracker crumbs

1 tablespoon sugar

5 tablespoons butter, melted

~ **VARIATION** ~

For Frozen Raspberry Pie, use raspberries in place of the strawberries and prepare the same way, or try other frozen fruit.

1 ▲ For the crust, mix together the crumbs, sugar, and butter.

2 Press the crumbs evenly and firmly over the bottom and sides of a 9-inch pie pan. Freeze until firm.

3 ▼ Blend together the cream cheese and sour cream. Set aside ½ cup of the strawberries and their juice. Add the rest to the cream cheese mixture.

4 Pour the filling into the crust and freeze 6–8 hours until firm. To serve, slice and spoon some of the reserved berries and juice on top.

Chocolate Cheesecake Pie (top), Frozen Strawberry Pie

Kiwi Ricotta Cheese Tart

SERVES 8

½ cup blanched almonds

½ cup plus 1 tablespoon sugar

4 cups ricotta cheese

1 cup whipping cream

1 egg

3 egg yolks

1 tablespoon flour

⅛ teaspoon salt

2 tablespoons rum

grated rind of 1 lemon

2½ tablespoons lemon juice

¼ cup honey

5 kiwi fruit

FOR THE CRUST

1¼ cups flour

1 tablespoon sugar

½ teaspoon salt

½ teaspoon baking powder

6 tablespoons cold butter, cut in pieces

1 egg yolk

3–4 tablespoons whipping cream

1 For the crust, sift the flour, sugar, salt, and baking powder into a bowl. Cut in the butter until the mixture resembles coarse crumbs. Mix the egg yolk and cream. Stir in just enough to bind the dough.

2 ▲ Transfer to a lightly floured surface, flatten slightly, wrap in wax paper, and refrigerate for 30 minutes. Preheat the oven to 425°F.

3 ▲ On a lightly floured surface, roll out the dough ⅛ inch thick and transfer to a 9-inch springform pan. Crimp the edge decoratively.

4 ▲ Prick the bottom of the dough all over with a fork. Line with crumpled wax paper and fill with pie weights. Bake for 10 minutes. Remove the paper and weights and bake until golden, 6–8 minutes more. Let cool. Reduce the heat to 350°F.

5 ▲ Grind the almonds finely with 1 tablespoon of the sugar in a food processor, blender, or nut grinder.

6 With an electric mixer, beat the ricotta until creamy. Add the cream, egg, yolks, remaining sugar, flour, salt, rum, lemon rind, and 2 tablespoons of the lemon juice. Beat to combine.

7 ▲ Stir in the ground almonds until well blended.

8 Pour into the shell and bake until golden, about 1 hour. Let cool, then refrigerate, loosely covered, for 2–3 hours. Unmold and place on a plate.

9 Combine the honey and remaining lemon juice for the glaze. Set aside.

10 ▲ Peel the kiwis. Halve them lengthwise, then cut crosswise into ¼-inch slices. Arrange the slices in rows across the top of the tart. Just before serving, brush with the glaze.

Apple Strudel

SERVES 10–12

½ cup raisins

2 tablespoons brandy

5 eating apples, such as Granny Smith or Jonathan

3 large, tart cooking apples

½ cup dark brown sugar, firmly packed

1 teaspoon ground cinnamon

grated rind and juice of 1 lemon

⅓ cup dry bread crumbs

½ cup pecans, chopped

12 sheets phyllo pastry

¾ cup (1½ sticks) butter, melted

confectioners' sugar, for dusting

whipped cream, for serving

1 Soak the raisins in the brandy for at least 15 minutes.

2 ▼ Peel, core, and thinly slice the apples. In a bowl, combine the sugar, cinnamon, and lemon rind. Stir in the apples, and half the bread crumbs.

3 Add the raisins, nuts and lemon juice and stir until blended.

4 Preheat the oven to 375°F. Grease 2 baking sheets.

5 ▲ Carefully unfold the phyllo sheets. Keep the unused sheets covered with wax paper. Lift off one sheet, place on a clean surface, and brush with melted butter. Lay a second sheet on top and brush with butter. Continue until you have a stack of 6 buttered sheets.

6 Sprinkle a few tablespoons of bread crumbs over the last sheet and spoon half the apple mixture at the bottom edge of the strip.

7 ▲ Starting at the apple-filled end, roll up the pastry, as for a jelly roll. Place on a baking sheet, seam-side down, and carefully fold under the ends to seal. Repeat the procedure to make a second strudel. Brush both with butter.

8 Bake the strudels for 45 minutes. Let cool slightly. Using a small sieve, dust with a fine layer of confectioners' sugar. Serve with whipped cream.

Cherry Strudel

SERVES 8

2 cups fresh bread crumbs
¾ cup (1½ sticks) butter, melted
1 cup sugar
1 tablespoon ground cinnamon
1 teaspoon grated lemon rind
4 cups sour cherries, pitted
8 sheets phyllo pastry
confectioners' sugar, for dusting

1 Lightly fry the bread crumbs in 5 tablespoons of the butter until golden. Set aside to cool.

2 ▲ In a large mixing bowl, toss together the sugar, cinnamon, and lemon rind.

3 Stir in the cherries.

4 Preheat the oven to 375°F. Grease a baking sheet.

5 Carefully unfold the phyllo sheets. Keep the unused sheets covered with wax paper. Lift off one sheet, place on a flat surface lined with wax paper. Brush the pastry with melted butter. Sprinkle bread crumbs evenly over the surface, using about ¼ cup of crumbs.

6 ▲ Lay a second sheet of phyllo on top, brush with butter and sprinkle with crumbs. Continue until you have a stack of 8 buttered sheets.

7 Spoon the cherry mixture at the bottom edge of the strip. Starting at the cherry-filled end, roll up the dough as for a jelly roll. Use the wax paper to help flip the strudel on to the baking sheet, seam-side down.

8 ▼ Carefully fold under the ends to seal in the fruit. Brush the top with any remaining butter.

9 Bake the strudel for 45 minutes. Let cool slightly. Using a small sieve, dust with a fine layer of confectioners' sugar. Serve warm.

Mushroom Quiche

SERVES 8

1 pound fresh mushrooms

2 tablespoons olive oil

1 tablespoon butter

1 clove garlic, finely chopped

1 tablespoon fresh lemon juice

salt and pepper

2 tablespoons finely chopped parsley

3 eggs

1½ cups whipping cream

½ cup freshly grated Parmesan cheese

FOR THE CRUST

1¼ cups flour

½ teaspoon salt

6 tablespoons cold butter, cut in pieces

3 tablespoons cold margarine, cut in pieces

3–4 tablespoons ice water

1 For the crust, sift the flour and salt into a bowl. Cut in the butter and margarine with a pastry blender until the mixture resembles coarse crumbs. Stir in just enough water to bind.

2 Gather into a ball, wrap in wax paper and refrigerate for 20 minutes.

3 Place a baking sheet in the center of the oven and preheat to 375°F.

4 Roll out the dough ⅛ inch thick and transfer to a 9-inch tart pan. Trim the edge. Prick the base all over with a fork. Line with crumpled wax paper and fill with pie weights. Bake for 12 minutes. Remove the paper and weights and continue baking until golden, about 5 minutes more.

5 ▲ Wipe the mushrooms with a damp paper towel to remove any dirt. Trim the ends of the stalks, place on a cutting board, and slice thinly.

6 Heat the oil and butter in a frying pan. Stir in the mushrooms, garlic, and lemon juice. Season with salt and pepper. Cook until the mushrooms render their liquid, then raise the heat and cook until dry.

7 ▼ Stir in the parsley and add more salt and pepper if necessary.

8 Whisk the eggs and cream together, then stir in the mushrooms. Sprinkle the cheese in the prebaked shell and pour the mushroom filling over the top.

9 Bake until puffed and brown, about 30 minutes. Serve the quiche warm.

Bacon and Cheese Quiche

SERVES 8

4 ounces medium-thick bacon slices

3 eggs

1½ cups whipping cream

1 cup grated Swiss cheese

⅛ teaspoon grated nutmeg

salt and pepper

FOR THE CRUST

1¼ cups flour

½ teaspoon salt

6 tablespoons cold butter, cut in pieces

3 tablespoons cold margarine, cut in pieces

3–4 tablespoons ice water

1 Make the crust as directed in steps 1–4 above. Maintain the oven temperature at 375°F.

2 ▲ Fry the bacon until crisp. Drain, then crumble into small pieces. Sprinkle in the pie shell.

3 ▲ Beat together the eggs, cream, cheese, nutmeg, salt, and pepper. Pour over the bacon and bake until puffed and brown, about 30 minutes. Serve the quiche warm.

Mushroom Quiche (top), Bacon and Cheese Quiche

Cheesy Tomato Quiche

SERVES 6–8

10 medium-sized tomatoes

1 2-ounce can anchovy fillets, drained and finely chopped

½ cup whipping cream

2 cups grated Monterey Jack cheese

¾ cup whole-wheat bread crumbs

½ teaspoon dried thyme

salt and pepper

FOR THE CRUST

1½ cups flour

½ cup (1 stick) cold butter, cut in pieces

1 egg yolk

2–3 tablespoons ice water

1 For the crust, sift the flour into a bowl. Cut in the butter with a pastry blender until the mixture resembles coarse crumbs.

2 ▲ With a fork, stir in the egg yolk and enough water to bind the dough.

3 Roll out the dough about ⅛ inch thick and transfer to a 9-inch tart pan. Refrigerate until needed. Preheat the oven to 400°F.

4 ▲ Score the bottoms of the tomatoes. Plunge in boiling water for 1 minute. Remove and peel off the skin with a knife. Cut in quarters and remove the seeds with a spoon.

5 ▲ In a bowl, mix the anchovies and cream. Stir in the cheese.

6 Sprinkle the bread crumbs in the tart. Arrange the tomatoes on top. Season with thyme, salt, and pepper.

7 ▲ Spoon the cheese mixture on top. Bake until golden, 25–30 minutes. Serve warm.

Onion and Anchovy Tart

SERVES 8

4 tablespoons olive oil

2 pounds onions, sliced

1 teaspoon dried thyme

salt and pepper

2–3 tomatoes, sliced

24 small black olives, pitted

1 2-ounce can anchovy fillets, drained and sliced

6 sun-dried tomatoes, cut into slivers

FOR THE CRUST

1¼ cups flour

½ teaspoon salt

½ cup (1 stick) cold butter, cut in pieces

1 egg yolk

2–3 tablespoons ice water

3 ▲ Heat the oil in a frying pan. Add the onions, thyme, and seasoning. Cook over low heat, covered, for 25 minutes. Uncover and continue cooking until soft. Let cool. Preheat the oven to 400°F.

4 ▼ Spoon the onions into the tart shell and top with the tomato slices. Arrange the olives in rows. Make a lattice pattern, alternating lines of anchovies and sun-dried tomatoes. Bake until golden, 20–25 minutes.

1 ▲ For the crust, sift the flour and salt into a bowl. Cut in the butter with a pastry blender until the mixture resembles coarse crumbs. Stir in the yolk and just enough water to bind.

2 ▲ Roll out the dough about ⅛ inch thick. Transfer to a 9-inch tart pan, using a rolling pin, and trim the edge. Refrigerate until needed.

Ricotta and Basil Tart

SERVES 8–10

2 cups basil leaves, tightly packed

1 cup flat-leaf parsley

½ cup extra-virgin olive oil

salt and pepper

2 eggs

1 egg yolk

1¾ pounds ricotta cheese

½ cup black olives, pitted

½ cup freshly grated Parmesan cheese

FOR THE CRUST

1¼ cups flour

½ teaspoon salt

6 tablespoons cold butter, cut in pieces

3 tablespoons cold margarine, cut in pieces

3–4 tablespoons ice water

1 ▲ For the crust, combine the flour and salt in a bowl. Add the butter and margarine.

2 Cut in with a pastry blender until the mixture resembles coarse crumbs. With a fork, stir in just enough water to bind the dough. Gather into a ball, wrap in wax paper, and refrigerate for at least 20 minutes.

3 Place a baking sheet in the center of the oven and preheat to 375°F.

4 Roll out the dough ⅛ inch thick and transfer to a 10-inch tart pan. Prick the base with a fork and line with crumpled wax paper. Fill with pie weights and bake for 12 minutes. Remove the paper and weights and bake until golden, 3–5 minutes more. Lower the heat to 350°F.

5 ▲ In a food processor, combine the basil, parsley, and olive oil. Season well with salt and pepper and process until finely chopped.

6 In a bowl, whisk the eggs and yolk to blend. Gently fold in the ricotta.

7 ▲ Fold in the basil mixture and olives until well combined. Stir in the Parmesan and adjust the seasoning.

8 Pour into the prebaked shell and bake until set, 30–35 minutes.

Pennsylvania Dutch Ham and Apple Pie

SERVES 6–8

5 tart cooking apples

4 tablespoons brown sugar, firmly packed

1 tablespoon flour

⅛ teaspoon ground cloves

⅛ teaspoon ground black pepper

6 ounces sliced baked ham

2 tablespoons butter or margarine

4 tablespoons whipping cream

1 egg yolk

FOR THE CRUST

2 cups flour

½ teaspoon salt

6 tablespoons cold butter, cut in pieces

4 tablespoons cold margarine, cut in pieces

¼–½ cup ice water

1 For the crust, sift the flour and salt into a bowl. Cut in the butter and margarine with a pastry blender until the mixture resembles coarse crumbs. Stir in enough water to bind, gather into 2 balls, and wrap in wax paper. Refrigerate for 20 minutes. Preheat the oven to 425°F.

2 ▲ Quarter, core, peel, and thinly slice the apples. Place in a bowl and toss with the sugar, flour, cloves, and pepper to coat evenly. Set aside.

3 Roll out one dough ball ⅛ inch thick and transfer to a 10-inch pie pan. Leave an overhang.

4 Arrange half the ham slices in the bottom. Top with a ring of apple slices. Dot with half the butter or margarine.

5 ▲ Repeat layering, finishing with apples. Dot with butter or margarine. Pour over 3 tablespoons of the cream.

6 Roll out the remaining dough and transfer to the top of the pie. Fold the top edge under the bottom crust and press to seal.

7 ▲ Roll out the dough scraps and stamp out decorative shapes. Arrange on top of the pie. Ruffle the edge using your finger and a fork. Cut steam vents at regular intervals. Mix the egg yolk and remaining cream and brush on top to glaze.

8 Bake for 10 minutes. Reduce the heat to 350°F and bake until golden, 30–35 minutes more. Serve hot.

CAKES & TORTES

~

As tasty as they are beautiful, with homespun charm or sophisticated style, these cakes and tortes make any occasion memorable. The special section of delightful party cakes takes the mystery out of cake decoration.

Angel Food Cake

SERVES 12–14

1 cup sifted cake flour
1½ cups superfine sugar
1¼ cups egg whites (about 10–11 eggs)
1¼ teaspoons cream of tartar
¼ teaspoon salt
1 teaspoon vanilla extract
¼ teaspoon almond extract
confectioners' sugar, for dusting

1 Preheat the oven to 325°F.

2 ▼ Sift the flour before measuring, then sift it **4** times with ½ cup of the sugar. Transfer to a bowl.

3 With an electric mixer, beat the egg whites until foamy. Sift over the cream of tartar and salt and continue to beat until they hold soft peaks when the beaters are lifted.

4 ▲ Add the remaining sugar in **3** batches, beating well after each addition. Stir in the vanilla and almond extracts.

5 ▲ Add the flour mixture, ½ cup at a time, and fold in with a large metal spoon after each addition.

6 Transfer to an ungreased 10-inch tube pan and bake until delicately browned on top, about 1 hour.

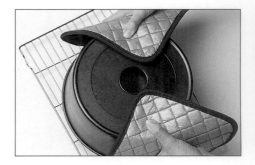

7 ▲ Turn the pan upside down onto a cake rack and let cool for 1 hour. If the cake does not unmold, run a spatula around the edge to loosen it. Invert on a serving plate.

8 When cool, lay a star-shaped template on top of the cake, sift over confectioners' sugar, and lift off.

Black and White Pound Cake

SERVES 16

4 1-ounce squares semisweet chocolate

3 cups flour

1 teaspoon baking powder

2 cups (4 sticks) butter, at room temperature

3⅓ cups sugar

1 tablespoon vanilla extract

10 eggs, at room temperature

confectioners' sugar, for dusting

1 ▲ Preheat the oven to 350°F. Line the bottom of a 10-inch tube pan with wax paper and grease. Dust with flour and spread evenly with a brush.

2 ▲ Melt the chocolate in the top of a double boiler, or in a heatproof bowl set over a pan of hot water. Stir occasionally. Set aside.

3 In a bowl, sift together the flour and baking powder. In another bowl, cream the butter, sugar, and vanilla with an electric mixer until light and fluffy. Add the eggs, 2 at a time, then gradually incorporate the flour mixture on low speed.

4 ▲ Spoon half of the batter into the prepared pan.

5 ▲ Stir the chocolate into the remaining batter, then spoon into the pan. With a metal spatula, swirl the two batters to create a marbled effect.

6 Bake until a cake tester inserted in the center comes out clean, about 1 hour 45 minutes. Cover with foil halfway through baking. Let stand 15 minutes, then unmold and transfer to a cooling rack. To serve, dust with confectioners' sugar.

Chiffon Cake

SERVES 16

2 cups flour

1 tablespoon baking powder

1 teaspoon salt

1½ cups sugar

½ cup vegetable oil

7 eggs, at room temperature, separated

¾ cup cold water

2 teaspoons vanilla extract

2 teaspoons grated lemon rind

½ teaspoon cream of tartar

FOR THE FROSTING

⅔ cup (10⅔ tablespoons) unsalted
 butter, at room temperature

5 cups confectioners' sugar

4 teaspoons instant coffee dissolved in 4
 tablespoons hot water

1 Preheat the oven to 325°F.

2 ▼ Sift the flour, baking powder, and salt into a bowl. Stir in 1 cup of the sugar. Make a well in the center and add in the following order: oil, egg yolks, water, vanilla, and lemon rind. Beat with a whisk or metal spoon until the mixture is smooth.

3 With an electric mixer, beat the egg whites with the cream of tartar until they hold soft peaks. Add the remaining ½ cup of sugar and beat until they hold stiff peaks.

4 ▲ Pour the flour mixture over the whites in 3 batches, folding well after each addition.

5 Transfer the batter to an ungreased 10- × 4-inch tube pan and bake until the top springs back when touched lightly, about 1 hour and 10 minutes.

6 ▲ When baked, remove from the oven and immediately hang the cake upside-down over the neck of a funnel or a narrow bottle. Let cool. To remove the cake, run a knife around the inside to loosen, then turn the pan over and tap the sides sharply. Invert the cake onto a serving plate.

7 For the frosting, beat together the butter and confectioners' sugar with an electric mixer until smooth. Add the coffee and beat until fluffy. With a metal spatula, spread over the sides and top of the cake.

Spice Cake

SERVES 10–12

1¼ cups milk
2 tablespoons dark corn syrup
2 teaspoons vanilla extract
¾ cup walnuts, chopped
¾ cup (1½ sticks) butter, at room temperature
1½ cups sugar
1 egg, at room temperature
3 egg yolks, at room temperature
2 cups flour
1 tablespoon baking powder
1 teaspoon grated nutmeg
1 teaspoon ground cinnamon
½ teaspoon ground cloves
¼ teaspoon ground ginger
¼ teaspoon ground allspice
FOR THE FROSTING
6 ounces cream cheese
2 tablespoons unsalted butter, at room temperature
1¾ cups confectioners' sugar
2 tablespoons finely chopped stem ginger
2 tablespoons syrup from stem ginger
stem ginger pieces, for decorating

1 Preheat the oven to 350°F. Line 3 8-inch cake pans with wax paper and grease. In a bowl, combine the milk, corn syrup, vanilla, and walnuts.

2 ▼ With an electric mixer, cream the butter and sugar until light and fluffy. Beat in the egg and egg yolks. Add the milk mixture and stir well.

3 Sift together the flour, baking powder and spices 3 times.

4 ▲ Add the flour mixture in 4 batches, and fold in carefully after each addition.

5 Divide the cake mixture between the pans. Bake until the cakes spring back when touched lightly, about 25 minutes. Let stand 5 minutes, then unmold and cool on a rack.

6 ▼ For the frosting, combine all the ingredients and beat with an electric mixer. Spread the frosting between the layers and over the top. Decorate with pieces of stem ginger.

Caramel Layer Cake

SERVES 8–10

2 cups cake flour

1½ teaspoons baking powder

¾ cup (1½ sticks) butter, at room temperature

¾ cup granulated sugar

4 eggs, at room temperature, beaten

1 teaspoon vanilla extract

8 tablespoons milk

whipped cream, for decorating

caramel threads, for decorating (optional, see below)

FOR THE FROSTING

1⅔ cups dark brown sugar, firmly packed

1 cup milk

2 tablespoons unsalted butter

3–5 tablespoons whipping cream

1 Preheat the oven to 350°F. Line 2 8-inch cake pans with wax paper and grease lightly.

2 ▲ Sift the flour and baking powder together 3 times. Set aside.

~ **COOK'S TIP** ~

To make caramel threads, combine ½ cup sugar and ¼ cup water in a heavy saucepan. Boil until light brown. Dip the pan in cold water to halt cooking. Trail from a spoon on an oiled baking sheet.

3 With an electric mixer, cream the butter and granulated sugar until light and fluffy.

4 ▲ Slowly mix in the beaten eggs. Add the vanilla. Fold in the flour mixture, alternating with the milk.

5 ▲ Divide the batter between the prepared pans and spread evenly, hollowing out the centers slightly.

6 Bake until the cakes pull away from the sides of the pan, about 30 minutes. Let stand 5 minutes, then unmold and transfer to a rack.

7 ▲ For the frosting, combine the brown sugar and milk in a saucepan.

8 Bring to a boil, then cover and cook for 3 minutes. Remove the lid and continue to boil, without stirring, until the mixture reaches 236°F on a sugar thermometer.

9 ▲ Immediately remove the pan from the heat and add the butter, but do not stir it in. Let cool until lukewarm, then beat until the mixture is smooth and creamy.

10 Stir in enough cream to obtain a spreadable consistency. If necessary, refrigerate to thicken more.

11 ▲ Spread a layer of frosting on top of one cake. Sandwich with the second cake, then spread the top and sides with the rest of the frosting and smooth the surface.

12 To decorate, pipe whipped cream rosettes around the edge. If using, place a mound of caramel threads in the center before serving.

Lady Baltimore Cake

SERVES 8–10

2½ cups flour

2½ teaspoons baking powder

½ teaspoon salt

4 eggs

1½ cups sugar

grated rind of 1 large orange

1 cup freshly squeezed orange juice

1 cup vegetable oil

FOR THE FROSTING

2 egg whites

1½ cup sugar

5 tablespoons cold water

¼ teaspoon cream of tartar

1 teaspoon vanilla extract

½ cup pecans, finely chopped

½ cup raisins, chopped

3 dried figs, finely chopped

18 pecan halves, for decorating

1 Preheat the oven to 350°F. Line 2 9-inch round cake pans with wax paper and grease.

2 In a bowl, sift together the flour, baking powder, and salt. Set aside.

3 ▲ With an electric mixer, beat the eggs and sugar until thick and lemon-colored. Beat in the orange rind and juice, then the oil.

4 On low speed beat in the flour mixture in 3 batches. Divide the batter between the prepared pans.

5 ▲ Bake until a cake tester inserted in the center comes out clean, about 30 minutes. Let stand 15 minutes. To unmold, run a knife around the inside edge, then transfer the cakes to racks to cool completely.

6 ▲ For the frosting, combine the egg whites, sugar, water, and cream of tartar in the top of a double boiler, or in a heatproof bowl set over boiling water. With an electric mixer, beat until glossy and thick. Off the heat, add the vanilla, and continue beating until thick. Fold in the pecans, raisins, and figs.

7 Spread a layer of frosting on top of one cake. Sandwich with the second cake, then spread the top and sides with the rest of the frosting. Arrange the pecan halves on top.

Carrot Cake with Maple Butter Frosting

SERVES 12

1 pound carrots, peeled

1½ cups flour

2 teaspoons baking powder

½ teaspoon baking soda

1 teaspoon salt

2 teaspoons ground cinnamon

4 eggs

2 teaspoons vanilla extract

1 cup dark brown sugar, firmly packed

½ cup granulated sugar

1¼ cups sunflower oil

1 cup walnuts, finely chopped

½ cup raisins

walnut halves, for decorating (optional)

FOR THE FROSTING

6 tablespoons unsalted butter, at room
   temperature

3 cups confectioners' sugar

¼ cup maple syrup

1 Preheat the oven to 350°F. Line an
11- × 8-inch rectangular baking pan
with wax paper and grease.

2 ▲ Grate the carrots and set aside.

3 Sift the flour, baking powder,
baking soda, salt, and cinnamon into
a bowl. Set aside.

4 With an electric mixer, beat the
eggs until blended. Add the vanilla,
sugars, and oil; beat to incorporate.
Add the dry ingredients, in 3 batches,
folding in well after each addition.

5 ▲ Add the carrots, walnuts, and
raisins and fold in thoroughly.

6 Pour the batter into the prepared
pan and bake until the cake springs
back when touched lightly, 40–45
minutes. Let stand 10 minutes, then
unmold and transfer to a rack.

7 ▼ For the frosting, cream the
butter with half the sugar until soft.
Add the syrup, then beat in the
remaining sugar until blended.

8 Spread the frosting over the top of
the cake. Using a metal spatula, make
decorative ridges across the top. Cut
into squares. Decorate with walnut
halves, if wished.

Cranberry Upside-Down Cake

SERVES 8

12–14 ounces fresh cranberries

4 tablespoons butter

⅔ cup sugar

FOR THE BATTER

⅔ cup flour

1 teaspoon baking powder

3 eggs

½ cup sugar

grated rind of 1 orange

3 tablespoons butter, melted

1 Preheat the oven to 350°F. Place a baking sheet on the middle shelf of the oven.

2 Wash the cranberries and pat dry. Thickly smear the butter on the base and sides of a 9- × 2-inch round cake pan. Add the sugar and swirl the pan to coat evenly.

3 ▲ Add the cranberries and spread in an even layer over the bottom of the pan.

4 For the batter, sift the flour and baking powder twice. Set aside.

5 ▲ Combine the eggs, sugar, and orange rind in a heatproof bowl set over a pan of hot but not boiling water. With an electric mixer, beat until the eggs leave a ribbon trail when the beaters are lifted.

6 Add the flour mixture in 3 batches, folding in well after each addition. Gently fold in the melted butter, then pour over the cranberries.

7 Bake for 40 minutes. Let cool for 5 minutes, then run a knife around the inside edge to loosen.

8 ▲ To unmold, while the cake is still warm place a flat plate on top of the pan, bottom-side up. Holding the pan and plate tightly together with potholders or oven gloves, quickly flip over. Carefully lift off the pan.

Pineapple Upside-Down Cake

SERVES 8

½ cup (1 stick) butter
1 cup dark brown sugar, firmly packed
1 16-ounce can pineapple slices, drained
4 eggs, separated
grated rind of 1 lemon
⅛ teaspoon salt
½ cup granulated sugar
¾ cup flour
1 teaspoon baking powder

1 Preheat the oven to 350°F.

2 Melt the butter in an ovenproof cast-iron skillet, about 10 inches in diameter. Remove 1 tablespoon of the melted butter and set aside.

3 ▲ Add the brown sugar to the skillet and stir until blended. Place the drained pineapple slices on top in one layer. Set aside.

4 In a bowl, whisk together the egg yolks, reserved butter, and lemon rind until well blended. Set aside.

5 ▼ With an electric mixer, beat the egg whites with the salt until stiff. Fold in the granulated sugar, 2 tablespoons at a time. Fold in the egg yolk mixture.

6 Sift the flour and baking powder together. Carefully fold into the egg mixture in 3 batches.

7 ▲ Pour the batter over the pineapple and smooth level.

8 Bake until a cake tester inserted in the center comes out clean, about 30 minutes.

9 While still hot, place a serving plate on top of the skillet, bottom-side up. Holding them tightly together with potholders or oven gloves, quickly flip over. Serve hot or cold.

~ VARIATION ~

For Dried Apricot Upside-Down Cake, replace the pineapple slices with 1½ cups of dried apricots. If they need softening, simmer the apricots in about ½ cup orange juice until plump and soft. Drain the apricots and discard any remaining cooking liquid.

Lemon Coconut Layer Cake

SERVES 8–10

1 cup flour
⅛ teaspoon salt
8 eggs
1¾ cups granulated sugar
1 tablespoon grated orange rind
grated rind of 2 lemons
juice of 1 lemon
½ cup shredded coconut
2 tablespoons cornstarch
1 cup water
6 tablespoons butter
FOR THE FROSTING
½ cup (1 stick) unsalted butter, at room temperature
1 cup confectioners' sugar
grated rind of 1 lemon
6–8 tablespoons fresh lemon juice
1 4-ounce can shredded coconut

1 Preheat the oven to 350°F. Line 3 8-inch cake pans with wax paper and grease. In a bowl, sift together the flour and salt and set aside.

2 ▲ Place 6 of the eggs in a large heatproof bowl set over hot water. With an electric mixer, beat until frothy. Gradually beat in ¾ cup of the granulated sugar until the mixture doubles in volume and is thick enough to leave a ribbon trail when the beaters are lifted, about 10 minutes.

3 ▲ Remove the bowl from the hot water. Fold in the orange rind, half the grated lemon rind, and 1 tablespoon of the lemon juice until blended. Fold in the coconut.

4 Sift over the flour mixture in 3 batches, folding in thoroughly after each addition.

5 ▲ Divide the mixture between the prepared pans

6 Bake until the cakes pull away from the sides of the pan, 25–30 minutes. Let stand 3–5 minutes, then unmold and transfer to a cooling rack.

7 In a bowl, blend the cornstarch with a little cold water to dissolve. Whisk in the remaining eggs just until blended. Set aside.

8 ▲ In a saucepan, combine the remaining lemon rind and juice, the water, remaining sugar, and butter.

9 Over a moderate heat, bring the mixture to a boil. Whisk in the eggs and cornstarch, and return to a boil. Whisk continuously until thick, about 5 minutes. Remove from the heat. Cover with wax paper to stop a skin forming and set aside.

10 ▲ For the frosting, cream the butter and confectioners' sugar until smooth. Stir in the lemon rind and enough lemon juice to obtain a thick, spreadable consistency.

11 Sandwich the 3 cake layers with the lemon custard mixture. Spread the frosting over the top and sides. Cover the cake with the coconut, pressing it in gently.

Lemon Yogurt Coffee Cake

SERVES 12

1 cup (2 sticks) butter, at room
temperature

1½ cups granulated sugar

4 eggs, at room temperature, separated

2 teaspoons grated lemon rind

⅓ cup fresh lemon juice

1 cup plain yogurt

2 cups flour

2 teaspoons baking powder

1 teaspoon baking soda

½ teaspoon salt

FOR THE GLAZE

1 cup confectioners' sugar

2 tablespoons fresh lemon juice

3–4 tablespoons plain yogurt

1 Preheat the oven to 350°F. Grease
a 12-cup bundt or tube pan and dust
with flour.

2 With an electric mixer, cream the
butter and granulated sugar until light
and fluffy. Add the egg yolks, 1 at a
time, beating well after each addition.

3 ▲ Add the lemon rind, juice, and
yogurt and stir to blend.

4 Sift together the flour, baking
powder, and baking soda. Set aside. In
another bowl, beat the egg whites and
salt until they hold stiff peaks.

5 ▲ Fold the dry ingredients into the
butter mixture, then fold in a dollop
of egg whites. Fold in the remaining
whites until blended.

6 Pour into the pan and bake until a
cake tester inserted in the center
comes out clean, about 50 minutes.
Let stand 15 minutes, then unmold
and transfer to a cooling rack.

7 For the glaze, sift the confectioners'
sugar into a bowl. Stir in the lemon
juice and just enough yogurt to make a
smooth glaze.

8 ▲ Set the cooled cake on a rack
over a sheet of wax paper or a baking
sheet. Pour over the glaze and let it
drip down the sides. Allow the glaze
to set before serving.

Sour Cream Streusel Coffee Cake

SERVES 12–14

½ cup (1 stick) butter, at room temperature

⅔ cup granulated sugar

3 eggs, at room temperature

1½ cups flour

1 teaspoon baking soda

1 teaspoon baking powder

1 cup sour cream

FOR THE TOPPING

1 cup dark brown sugar, firmly packed

2 teaspoons ground cinnamon

1 cup walnuts, finely chopped

4 tablespoons cold butter, cut in pieces

1 Preheat the oven to 350°F. Line the bottom of a 9-inch square cake pan with wax paper and grease.

2 ▲ For the topping, place the brown sugar, cinnamon, and walnuts in a bowl. Mix with your fingertips, then add the butter and continue working with your fingertips until the mixture resembles coarse crumbs.

3 To make the cake, cream the butter with an electric mixer until soft. Add the sugar and continue beating until the mixture is light and fluffy.

4 Add the eggs, 1 at a time, beating well after each addition.

5 In another bowl, sift the flour, baking soda, and baking powder together 3 times.

6 ▲ Fold the dry ingredients into the butter mixture in 3 batches, alternating with the sour cream. Fold until blended after each addition.

7 ▲ Pour half of the batter into the prepared pan and sprinkle over half of the walnut topping mixture.

8 Pour the remaining batter on top and sprinkle over the remaining walnut mixture.

9 Bake until browned, 60–70 minutes. Let stand 5 minutes, then unmold and transfer to a cooling rack.

Plum Crumbcake

SERVES 8–10

⅔ cup (10⅔ tablespoons) butter or margarine, at room temperature

⅔ cup granulated sugar

4 eggs, at room temperature

1½ teaspoons vanilla extract

1¼ cups flour

1 teaspoon baking powder

1½ pounds purple plums, halved and pitted

FOR THE TOPPING

1 cup flour

⅔ cup light brown sugar, firmly packed

1½ teaspoons ground cinnamon

6 tablespoons butter, cut in pieces

1 Preheat the oven to 350°F.

2 For the topping, combine the flour, light brown sugar, and cinnamon in a bowl. Add the butter and work the mixture lightly with your fingertips until it resembles coarse crumbs. Set aside.

3 ▲ Line a 10- × 2-inch round cake pan with wax paper and grease.

4 Cream the butter or margarine and granulated sugar until light and fluffy.

5 ▲ Beat in the eggs, 1 at a time. Stir in the vanilla.

6 In a bowl, sift together the flour and baking powder, then fold into the butter mixture in 3 batches.

7 ▲ Pour the batter into the pan. Arrange the plums on top.

8 ▲ Sprinkle the topping over the plums in an even layer.

9 Bake until a cake tester inserted in the center comes out clean, about 45 minutes. Let cool in the pan.

10 To serve, run a knife around the inside edge and invert onto a plate. Invert again onto a serving plate so the topping is right-side up.

~ VARIATION ~

This cake can also be made with the same quantity of apricots, peeled if preferred, or pitted cherries, or use a mixture of fruit, such as red or yellow plums, greengage plums, and apricots.

Peach Torte

SERVES 8

1 cup flour
1 teaspoon baking powder
⅛ teaspoon salt
½ cup (1 stick) unsalted butter, at room temperature
¾ cup sugar
2 eggs, at room temperature
6–7 peaches
sugar and lemon juice, for sprinkling
whipped cream, for serving (optional)

1 Preheat the oven to 350°F. Grease a 10-inch springform pan.

2 ▲ Sift together the flour, baking powder, and salt. Set aside.

3 With an electric mixer, cream the butter and sugar until light and fluffy. Add the eggs, then fold in the dry ingredients until blended.

4 ▲ Spoon the batter into the pan and smooth it to make an even layer over the bottom.

5 ▼ To skin the peaches, drop several at a time into a pan of gently boiling water. Boil for 10 seconds, then remove with a slotted spoon. Peel off the skin with the aid of a sharp knife. Cut the peaches in half and discard the stones.

6 ▲ Arrange the peach halves on top of the batter. Sprinkle lightly with sugar and lemon juice.

7 Bake until golden brown and set, 50–60 minutes. Serve warm with whipped cream, if desired.

Apple Ring Cake

SERVES 12

7 eating apples, such as Jonathan or
  Granny Smith

1½ cups vegetable oil

2 cups sugar

3 eggs

3 cups flour

1 teaspoon salt

1 teaspoon baking soda

1 teaspoon ground cinnamon

1 teaspoon vanilla extract

1 cup walnuts, chopped

1 cup raisins

confectioners' sugar, for dusting

1 Preheat the oven to 350°F. Grease
a 9-inch tube pan.

2 ▲ Quarter, peel, core, and slice
the apples into a bowl. Set aside.

3 With an electric mixer, beat the oil
and sugar together until blended. Add
the eggs and continue beating until
the mixture is creamy.

4 Sift together the flour, salt, baking
soda, and cinnamon.

5 ▼ Fold the flour mixture into the
egg mixture with the vanilla. Stir in
the apples, walnuts, and raisins.

6 Pour into the pan and bake until
the cake springs back when touched
lightly, about 1¼ hours. Let stand 15
minutes, then unmold and transfer to
a cooling rack. Dust with a layer of
confectioners' sugar before serving.

Orange Cake

SERVES 6

1¼ cups flour

1½ teaspoons baking powder

⅛ teaspoon salt

½ cup (1 stick) butter or margarine

½ cup sugar

grated rind of 1 large orange

2 eggs, at room temperature

2 tablespoons milk

FOR THE SYRUP AND DECORATION

½ cup sugar

1 cup fresh orange juice, strained

3 orange slices, for decorating

1 Preheat the oven to 350°F. Line an
8-inch cake pan with wax paper and
grease.

2 ▲ Sift the flour, salt, and baking
powder onto a square of wax paper.

3 With an electric mixer, cream the
butter or margarine until soft. Add the
sugar and orange rind and continue
beating until light and fluffy. Beat in
the eggs, 1 at a time. Fold in the flour
in 3 batches, then add the milk.

4 Spoon into the pan and bake until
the cake pulls away from the sides,
about 30 minutes. Remove from the
oven but leave in the pan.

5 Meanwhile, for the syrup, dissolve
the sugar in the orange juice over low
heat. Add the orange slices and
simmer for 10 minutes. Remove and
drain. Let the syrup cool.

6 ▲ Prick the cake all over with a
fine skewer. Pour the syrup over the
hot cake. It may seem at first that
there is too much syrup for the cake to
absorb, but it will soak it all up.
Unmold when completely cooled and
decorate with small triangles of the
orange slices arranged on top.

Apple Ring Cake (top), Orange Cake

Orange Walnut Roll

SERVES 8

4 eggs, separated

½ cup sugar

1 cup walnuts, chopped very finely

⅛ teaspoon cream of tartar

⅛ teaspoon salt

confectioners' sugar, for dusting

FOR THE FILLING

1¼ cups whipping cream

1 tablespoon granulated sugar

grated rind of 1 orange

1 tablespoon orange liqueur, such as
    Grand Marnier

1 Preheat the oven to 350°F. Line a
12- × 9½-inch jelly roll pan with wax
paper and grease.

2 With an electric mixer, beat the
egg yolks and sugar until thick.

3 ▲ Stir in the walnuts.

4 In another bowl, beat the egg
whites with the cream of tartar and
salt until they hold stiff peaks. Fold
gently but thoroughly into the
walnut mixture.

5 Pour the batter into the prepared
pan and spread level with a spatula.
Bake for 15 minutes.

6 Run a knife along the inside edge to
loosen, then invert the cake onto a
sheet of wax paper that has been
dusted with confectioners' sugar.

7 ▲ Peel off the baking paper. Roll
up the cake while it is still warm with
the help of the sugared paper. Set
aside to cool.

8 For the filling, whip the cream
until it holds soft peaks. Stir together
the granulated sugar and orange rind,
then fold into the whipped cream.
Add the liqueur.

9 ▲ Gently unroll the cake. Spread
the inside with a layer of orange
whipped cream, then re-roll. Keep
refrigerated until ready to serve. Dust
the top with confectioners' sugar just
before serving.

Chocolate Roll

SERVES 10

8 1-ounce squares semisweet chocolate
3 tablespoons water
2 tablespoons rum, brandy, or strong coffee
7 eggs, separated
¾ cup sugar
⅛ teaspoon salt
1½ cups whipping cream
confectioners' sugar, for dusting

1 Preheat the oven to 350°F. Line a 15- × 13-inch jelly roll pan with wax paper and grease.

2 ▲ Combine the chocolate, water, and rum or other flavoring in the top of a double boiler, or in a heatproof bowl set over hot water. Heat until melted. Set aside.

3 With an electric mixer, beat the egg yolks and sugar until thick.

4 ▲ Stir in the melted chocolate.

5 In another bowl, beat the egg whites and salt until they hold stiff peaks. Fold a large dollop of egg whites into the yolk mixture to lighten it, then carefully fold in the rest of the whites.

6 ▼ Pour the batter into the pan; spread evenly with a metal spatula.

7 Bake for 15 minutes. Remove from the oven, cover with wax paper and a damp cloth. Let stand for 1–2 hours.

8 With an electric mixer, whip the cream until stiff. Set aside.

9 Run a knife along the inside edge to loosen, then invert the cake onto a sheet of wax paper that has been dusted with confectioners' sugar.

10 Peel off the baking paper. Spread with an even layer of whipped cream, then roll up the cake with the help of the sugared paper. The cake may crack slightly.

11 Refrigerate for several hours. Before serving, dust with an even layer of confectioners' sugar.

Chocolate Frosted Layer Cake

SERVES 8

1 cup (2 sticks) butter or margarine, at room temperature

1½ cups sugar

4 eggs, at room temperature, separated

2 teaspoons vanilla extract

2½ cups flour

2 teaspoons baking powder

⅛ teaspoon salt

1 cup milk

FOR THE FROSTING

5 1-ounce squares semisweet chocolate

½ cup sour cream

⅛ teaspoon salt

1 Preheat the oven to 350°F. Line 2 8-inch round cake pans with wax paper and grease. Coat the pans with flour and shake to distribute evenly. Tap to dislodge any excess flour.

2 With an electric mixer, cream the butter or margarine until soft. Gradually add the sugar and continue beating until light and fluffy.

3 ▲ Lightly beat the egg yolks, then mix into the creamed butter and sugar with the vanilla.

4 Sift the flour with the baking powder 3 times. Set aside.

5 In another bowl, beat the egg whites with the salt until they hold stiff peaks. Set aside.

6 ▲ Gently fold the dry ingredients into the butter mixture in 3 batches, alternating with the milk.

7 Add a large dollop of the whites and fold in to lighten the mixture. Carefully fold in the remaining whites until just blended.

8 Divide the batter between the pans and bake until the cakes pull away from the sides of the pan, about 30 minutes. Let stand 5 minutes, then unmold and transfer to a rack.

9 ▲ For the frosting, melt the chocolate in the top of a double boiler or a bowl set over hot water. When cool, stir in the sour cream and salt.

10 Sandwich the layers with frosting, then spread on the top and sides.

Devil's Food Cake with Orange Frosting

SERVES 8–10

½ cup unsweetened cocoa powder
¾ cup boiling water
¾ cup (1½ sticks) butter, at room temperature
1½ cups dark brown sugar, firmly packed
3 eggs, at room temperature
2 cups flour
1½ teaspoons baking soda
¼ teaspoon baking powder
¾ cup sour cream
orange rind strips, for decoration
FOR THE FROSTING
1½ cups granulated sugar
2 egg whites
4 tablespoons frozen orange juice concentrate
1 tablespoon fresh lemon juice
grated rind of 1 orange

1 Preheat the oven to 350°F. Line 2 9-inch cake pans with wax paper and grease. In a bowl, mix the cocoa and water until smooth. Set aside.

2 With an electric mixer, cream the butter and sugar until light and fluffy. Add the eggs, 1 at a time, beating well after each addition.

3 ▲ When the cocoa mixture is lukewarm, add to the butter mixture.

4 ▼ Sift together the flour, baking soda, and baking powder twice. Fold into the cocoa mixture in 3 batches, alternating with the sour cream.

5 Pour into the pans and bake until the cakes pull away from the sides of the pan, 30–35 minutes. Let stand 15 minutes before unmolding.

6 Thinly slice the orange rind strips. Blanch in boiling water for 1 minute.

7 ▲ For the frosting, place all the ingredients in the top of a double boiler or in a bowl set over hot water. With an electric mixer, beat until the mixture holds soft peaks. Continue beating off the heat until thick enough to spread.

8 Sandwich the cake layers with frosting, then spread over the top and sides. Arrange the blanched orange rind strips on top of the cake.

Best-Ever Chocolate Cake

SERVES 12–14

½ cup (1 stick) unsalted butter
1 cup cake flour
½ cup unsweetened cocoa powder
1 teaspoon baking powder
⅛ teaspoon salt
6 eggs
1 cup sugar
2 teaspoons vanilla extract
FOR THE FROSTING
8 1-ounce squares semisweet chocolate, chopped
6 tablespoons unsalted butter
3 eggs, separated
1 cup whipping cream
3 tablespoons sugar

1 Preheat the oven to 350°F. Line 3 8- × 1½-inch round cake pans with wax paper and grease.

2 ▲ Dust evenly with flour and spread with a brush. Set aside.

~ **VARIATION** ~

For a simpler frosting, combine 1 cup whipping cream with 8 ounces finely chopped semisweet chocolate in a saucepan. Stir over low heat until the chocolate has melted. Cool and whisk to spreading consistency.

3 ▲ Melt the butter over low heat. With a spoon, skim off any foam that rises to the surface. Set aside.

4 ▲ Sift the flour, cocoa, baking powder, and salt together 3 times and set aside.

5 Place the eggs and sugar in a large heatproof bowl set over a pan of hot water. With an electric mixer, beat until the mixture doubles in volume and is thick enough to leave a ribbon trail when the beaters are lifted, about 10 minutes. Add the vanilla.

6 ▲ Sift over the dry ingredients in 3 batches, folding in carefully after each addition. Fold in the butter.

7 Divide the batter between the pans and bake until the cakes pull away from the sides of the pan, about 25 minutes. Transfer to a rack.

8 For the frosting, melt the chopped chocolate in the top of a double boiler, or in a heatproof bowl set over hot water.

9 ▲ Off the heat, stir in the butter and egg yolks. Return to low heat and stir until thick. Remove from the heat and set aside.

10 Whip the cream until firm; set aside. In another bowl, beat the egg whites until stiff. Add the sugar and beat until glossy.

11 Fold the cream into the chocolate mixture, then carefully fold in the egg whites. Refrigerate for 20 minutes to thicken the frosting.

12 ▲ Sandwich the cake layers with frosting, stacking them carefully. Spread the remaining frosting evenly over the top and sides of the cake.

Rich Chocolate Pecan Cake

1 cup (2 sticks) butter
8 1-ounce squares semisweet chocolate
1 cup unsweetened cocoa powder
1½ cups sugar
6 eggs
⅓ cup brandy or cognac
2 cups pecans, finely chopped

FOR THE GLAZE

4 tablespoons butter
5 1-ounce squares bittersweet chocolate
2 tablespoons milk
1 teaspoon vanilla extract

1 Preheat the oven to 350°F. Line a 9- × 2-inch round cake pan with wax paper and grease.

2 Melt the butter and chocolate together in the top of a double boiler, or in a heatproof bowl set over hot water. Set aside to cool.

3 ▼ Sift the cocoa into a bowl. Add the sugar and eggs and stir until just combined. Pour in the melted chocolate mixture and brandy.

4 Fold in three-quarters of the pecans, then pour the batter into the prepared pan.

5 ▲ Set the pan inside a large pan and pour 1 inch of hot water into the outer pan. Bake until the cake is firm to the touch, about 45 minutes. Let stand 15 minutes, then unmold and transfer to a cooling rack.

6 Wrap the cake in wax paper and refrigerate for at least 6 hours.

7 For the glaze, combine the butter, chocolate, milk, and vanilla in the top of a double boiler or in a heatproof bowl set over hot water, until melted.

8 Place a piece of wax paper under the cake, then drizzle spoonfuls of glaze along the edge; it should drip down and coat the sides. Pour the remaining glaze on top of the cake.

9 ▲ Cover the sides of the cake with the remaining pecans, gently pressing them on with the palm of your hand.

Chocolate Brownie Cake

SERVES 8–10

4 1-ounce squares unsweetened chocolate	
¾ cup (1½ sticks) butter	
2 cups sugar	
3 eggs	
1 teaspoon vanilla extract	
1½ cups flour	
1 teaspoon baking powder	
1 cup walnuts, chopped	
FOR THE TOPPING	
1½ cups whipping cream	
8 1-ounce squares semisweet chocolate	
1 tablespoon vegetable oil	

1 Preheat the oven to 350°F. Line 2 8-inch cake pans with wax paper and grease the paper.

2 Melt the chocolate and butter together in the top of a double boiler, or in a heatproof bowl set over a saucepan of hot water.

3 ▲ Transfer to a mixing bowl and stir in the sugar. Add the eggs and vanilla and mix until well blended.

~ **VARIATION** ~

To make Chocolate Brownie Ice Cream Cake, sandwich the cake layers with softened vanilla ice cream. Freeze until serving.

4 ▲ Sift over the flour and baking powder. Stir in the walnuts.

5 Divide the batter between the prepared pans and spread level.

6 Bake until a cake tester inserted in the center comes out clean, about 30 minutes. Let stand 10 minutes, then unmold and transfer to a rack.

7 When the cakes are cool, whip the cream until firm. With a long serrated knife, carefully slice each cake in half horizontally.

8 Sandwich the layers with some of the whipped cream and spread the remainder over the top of the cake. Refrigerate until needed.

9 ▼ For the chocolate curls, melt the chocolate and oil in the top of a double boiler or a bowl set over hot water. Transfer to a non-porous surface. Spread to a ⅜-inch thick rectangle. Just before the chocolate sets, hold the blade of a straight knife at an angle to the chocolate and scrape across the surface to make curls. Place on top of the cake.

Sachertorte

SERVES 8–10

2 1-ounce squares semisweet chocolate

2 1-ounce squares unsweetened chocolate

6 tablespoons unsalted butter, at room temperature

½ cup sugar

4 eggs, separated

1 egg white

¼ teaspoon salt

½ cup cake flour, sifted

FOR THE TOPPING

5 tablespoons apricot jam

1 cup plus 1 tablespoon water

1 tablespoon unsalted butter

6 1-ounce squares semisweet chocolate

¾ cup sugar

ready-made chocolate decorating icing (optional)

1 Preheat the oven to 325°F. Line a 9- × 2-inch cake pan with wax paper and grease.

2 ▲ Melt both chocolates in the top of a double boiler, or in a heatproof bowl set over hot water. Set aside.

3 With an electric mixer, cream the butter and sugar until light and fluffy. Stir in the chocolate.

4 ▲ Beat in the yolks, 1 at a time.

5 In another bowl, beat the egg whites with the salt until stiff.

6 ▲ Fold a dollop of whites into the chocolate mixture to lighten it. Fold in the remaining whites in 3 batches, alternating with the sifted flour.

7 ▲ Pour into the pan and bake until a cake tester comes out clean, about 45 minutes. Unmold onto a rack.

8 ▲ Meanwhile, melt the jam with 1 tablespoon of the water over low heat, then strain for a smooth consistency.

9 For the frosting, melt the butter and chocolate in the top of a double boiler or a bowl set over hot water.

10 ▲ In a heavy saucepan, dissolve the sugar in the remaining water over low heat. Raise the heat and boil until the mixture reaches 221°F on a sugar thermometer. Immediately plunge the bottom of the pan into cold water for 1 minute. Pour into the chocolate mixture and stir to blend. Let cool for a few minutes before using.

11 To assemble, brush the warm jam over the cake. Starting in the center, pour over the frosting and work outward in a circular movement. Tilt the rack to spread; only use a spatula for the sides of the cake. Leave to set overnight. If wished, decorate with chocolate icing.

Raspberry-Hazelnut Meringue Cake

SERVES 8

1 cup hazelnuts
4 egg whites
⅛ teaspoon salt
1 cup sugar
½ teaspoon vanilla extract
FOR THE FILLING
1¼ cups whipping cream
1½ pounds raspberries, about 3 pints

1 Preheat the oven to 350°F. Line the bottom of 2 8-inch cake pans with wax paper and grease.

2 Spread the hazelnuts on a baking sheet and bake until lightly toasted, about 8 minutes. Let cool slightly.

3 ▲ Rub the hazelnuts vigorously in a clean dish towel to remove most of the skins.

4 Grind the nuts in a food processor, blender, or nut grinder until they are the consistency of coarse sand.

5 Reduce the oven heat to 300°F.

6 With an electric mixer, beat the egg whites and salt until they hold stiff peaks. Beat in 2 tablespoons of the sugar, then fold in the remaining sugar, a few tablespoons at a time, with a rubber spatula. Fold in the vanilla and the hazelnuts.

7 ▲ Divide the batter between the prepared pans and spread level.

8 Bake for 1¼ hours. If the meringues brown too quickly, protect with a sheet of foil. Let stand 5 minutes, then carefully run a knife around the inside edge of the pans to loosen. Transfer to a rack to cool.

9 For the filling, whip the cream just until firm.

10 ▲ Spread half the cream in an even layer on one meringue round and top with half the raspberries.

11 Top with the other meringue round. Spread the remaining cream on top and arrange the remaining raspberries over the cream. Refrigerate for 1 hour to facilitate cutting.

Forgotten Torte

SERVES 6

6 egg whites, at room temperature

½ teaspoon cream of tartar

⅛ teaspoon salt

1½ cups granulated sugar

1 teaspoon vanilla extract

¾ cup whipping cream

FOR THE SAUCE

12 ounces fresh or thawed frozen raspberries

2–3 tablespoons confectioners' sugar

1 Preheat the oven to 450°F. Generously grease a 6-cup ring mold.

2 ▲ With an electric mixer, beat the egg whites, cream of tartar, and salt until they hold soft peaks. Gradually add the sugar and beat until glossy and stiff. Fold in the vanilla.

3 ▲ Spoon into the prepared pan and smooth the top level.

4 Place in the oven, then turn the oven off. Leave overnight; do not open the oven door at any time.

5 ▼ To serve, gently loosen the edge with a sharp knife and unmold onto a serving plate. Whip the cream until firm. Spread it over the top and upper sides of the meringue and decorate with any meringue crumbs.

6 ▲ For the sauce, purée the fruit, then strain. Sweeten to taste.

~ COOK'S TIP ~

This recipe is not suitable for fan-assisted and solid fuel ovens.

Pecan-Apple Torte

SERVES 8

1 cup pecan halves

½ cup flour

2 teaspoons baking powder

¼ teaspoon salt

2 large cooking apples

3 eggs

1 cup sugar

1 teaspoon vanilla extract

¾ cup whipping cream

1 Preheat the oven to 325°F. Line 2 9-inch cake pans with wax paper and grease. Spread the pecans on a baking sheet and bake for 10 minutes.

2 Finely chop the pecans. Reserve 1½ tablespoons and place the rest in a mixing bowl. Sift over the flour, baking powder, and salt and stir.

3 ▲ Quarter, core, and peel the apples. Cut into ⅛-inch dice, then stir into the pecan-flour mixture.

4 ▲ With an electric mixer, beat the eggs until frothy. Gradually add the sugar and vanilla and beat until a ribbon forms, about 8 minutes. Gently fold in the flour mixture.

5 Pour into the pans and level the tops. Bake until a cake tester inserted in the center comes out clean, about 35 minutes. Let stand 10 minutes.

6 ▲ To loosen, run a knife around the inside edge of each pan. Let cool.

7 ▲ Whip the cream until firm. Spread half over the cake. Top with the second cake. Pipe whipped cream rosettes on top and sprinkle over the reserved pecans before serving.

Almond Cake

SERVES 4–6

| 1½ cups blanched whole almonds, plus more for decorating |
| 2 tablespoons butter |
| ¾ cup confectioners' sugar |
| 3 eggs |
| ½ teaspoon almond extract |
| ¼ cup flour |
| 3 egg whites |
| 1 tablespoon granulated sugar |

1 ▲ Preheat the oven to 325°F. Line a 9-inch round cake pan with wax paper and grease.

2 ▲ Spread the almonds in a baking tray and toast for 10 minutes. Cool, then coarsely chop 1½ cups.

3 Melt the butter and set aside.

4 Preheat the oven to 400°F.

5 Grind the chopped almonds with half the confectioners' sugar in a food processor, blender, or nut grinder. Transfer to a mixing bowl.

6 ▲ Add the whole eggs and remaining confectioners' sugar. With an electric mixer, beat until the mixture forms a ribbon when the beaters are lifted. Mix in the butter and almond extract. Sift over the flour and fold in gently.

7 With an electric mixer, beat the egg whites until they hold soft peaks. Add the granulated sugar and beat until stiff and glossy.

8 ▲ Fold the whites into the almond mixture in 4 batches.

9 Spoon the batter into the prepared pan and bake in the center of the oven until golden brown, about 15–20 minutes. Decorate the top with the remaining toasted whole almonds. Serve warm.

Walnut Coffee Torte

SERVES 8–10

1¼ cups walnuts
¾ cup sugar
5 eggs, separated
⅓ cup dry bread crumbs
1 tablespoon unsweetened cocoa powder
1 tablespoon instant coffee
2 tablespoons rum or lemon juice
⅛ teaspoon salt
6 tablespoons concord grape or red currant jelly
chopped walnuts, for decorating
FOR THE FROSTING
8 1-ounce squares bittersweet chocolate
3 cups whipping cream

1 ▲ For the frosting, combine the chocolate and cream in the top of a double boiler, or in a heatproof bowl set over simmering water. Stir until the chocolate dissolves. Let cool, then cover and refrigerate until the mixture is firm, or overnight.

2 Preheat the oven to 350°F. Line a 9- × 2-inch cake pan with wax paper and grease.

3 ▲ Grind the nuts with 3 tablespoons of the sugar in a food processor, blender, or nut grinder.

4 With an electric mixer, beat the egg yolks and remaining sugar until thick and lemon-colored.

5 ▲ Fold in the walnuts. Stir in the bread crumbs, cocoa, coffee, and rum or lemon juice.

6 ▲ In another bowl, beat the egg whites with the salt until they hold stiff peaks. Fold carefully into the walnut mixture with a rubber spatula.

7 Pour the meringue batter into the prepared pan and bake until the top of the cake springs back when touched lightly, about 45 minutes. Let the cake stand for 5 minutes, then unmold and transfer to a rack.

8 ▲ When cool, slice the cake in half horizontally.

9 With an electric mixer, beat the chocolate frosting mixture on low speed until it becomes lighter, about 30 seconds. Do not overbeat or it may become grainy.

10 ▲ Warm the jelly in a saucepan until melted, then brush over the cut cake layer. Spread with some of the chocolate frosting, then sandwich with the remaining cake layer. Brush the top of the cake with jelly, then cover the sides and top with the remaining chocolate frosting. Make a starburst pattern by pressing gently with a table knife in lines radiating from the center. Sprinkle the chopped walnuts around the edge.

Light Fruit Cake

MAKES 2 LOAVES

8 ounces ready-to-eat prunes

8 ounces dates

8 ounces currants

8 ounces golden raisins

1 cup dry white wine

1 cup rum

3 cups flour

2 teaspoons baking powder

1 teaspoon ground cinnamon

½ teaspoon grated nutmeg

1 cup (2 sticks) butter, at room temperature

1 cup sugar

4 eggs, at room temperature, lightly beaten

1 teaspoon vanilla extract

1 Pit the prunes and dates and chop finely. Place in a bowl with the currants and raisins.

2 ▲ Stir in the wine and rum and let stand, covered, for 48 hours. Stir occasionally.

3 Preheat the oven to 300°F. Line 2 9- × 5- × 3-inch pans with wax paper and grease. Place a tray of hot water on the bottom of the oven.

4 Sift together the flour, baking powder, cinnamon, and nutmeg.

5 ▲ With an electric mixer, cream the butter and sugar together until light and fluffy.

6 Gradually add the eggs and vanilla. Fold in the flour mixture in 3 batches. Fold in the dried fruit mixture and its macerating liquid.

7 ▲ Divide the batter between the pans and bake until a cake tester inserted in the center comes out clean, about 1½ hours.

8 Let stand 20 minutes, then unmold and transfer to a cooling rack. Wrap in foil or wax paper and store in an airtight container. If possible, leave for at least 1 week before serving to allow the flavors to mellow.

Dark Fruit Cake

SERVES 12

1 cup currants

1 cup raisins

⅔ cup golden raisins

¼ cup candied cherries, halved

3 tablespoons Madeira or sherry wine

¾ cup (1½ sticks) butter

1 cup dark brown sugar, firmly packed

2 extra-large eggs, at room temperature

1⅔ cups flour

2 teaspoons baking powder

2 teaspoons each ground ginger, allspice, and cinnamon

1 tablespoon dark corn syrup

1 tablespoon milk

¼ cup mixed candied fruit, chopped

1 cup walnuts or pecans, chopped

FOR THE DECORATION

1 cup sugar

½ cup water

1 lemon, thinly sliced

½ orange, thinly sliced

½ cup orange marmalade

candied cherries

1 One day before preparing, combine the currants, both raisins, and the cherries in a bowl. Stir in the Madeira or sherry. Cover and let stand overnight to macerate.

2 Preheat the oven to 300°F. Line a 9- × 3-inch springform pan with wax paper and grease. Place a tray of hot water on the bottom of the oven.

3 With an electric mixer, cream the butter and sugar until light and fluffy. Beat in the eggs, 1 at a time.

4 ▲ Sift the flour, baking powder, and spices together 3 times. Fold into the butter mixture in 3 batches. Fold in the corn syrup, milk, dried fruit and liquid, candied fruit, and nuts.

5 ▲ Spoon into the pan, spreading out so there is a slight depression in the center of the batter.

6 Bake until a cake tester inserted in the center comes out clean, 2½–3 hours. Cover with foil when the top is golden to prevent overbrowning. Cool in the pan on a rack.

7 ▲ For the decoration, combine the sugar and water in a saucepan and bring to a boil. Add the lemon and orange slices and cook until candied, about 20 minutes. Work in batches, if necessary. Remove the fruit with a slotted spoon. Pour the remaining syrup over the cake and let cool. Melt the marmalade over low heat, then brush over the top of the cake. Decorate with the candied citrus slices and cherries.

Whiskey Cake

MAKES 1 LOAF

1½ cups walnuts, chopped

½ cup raisins, chopped

½ cup currants

1 cup flour

1 teaspoon baking powder

¼ teaspoon salt

½ cup (1 stick) butter

1 cup sugar

3 eggs, at room temperature, separated

1 teaspoon grated nutmeg

½ teaspoon ground cinnamon

⅓ cup bourbon whiskey

confectioners' sugar, for dusting

1 ▼ Preheat the oven to 325°F. Line the bottom of a 9- × 5- × 3-inch loaf pan with wax paper and grease the paper and sides of the pan.

2 ▲ Place the walnuts, raisins, and currants in a bowl. Sprinkle over 2 tablespoons of the flour, mix and set aside. Sift together the remaining flour, baking powder, and salt.

3 ▲ Cream the butter and sugar until light and fluffy. Beat in the egg yolks.

4 Mix the nutmeg, cinnamon, and whiskey. Fold into the butter mixture, alternating with the flour mixture.

5 ▲ In another bowl, beat the egg whites until stiff. Fold into the whiskey mixture until just blended. Fold in the walnut mixture.

6 Bake until a cake tester inserted in the center comes out clean, about 1 hour. Let cool in the pan. Dust with confectioners' sugar over a template.

Gingerbread

SERVES 8–10

1 tablespoon vinegar
¾ cup milk
1½ cups flour
2 teaspoons baking powder
¼ teaspoon baking soda
½ teaspoon salt
2 teaspoons ground ginger
1 teaspoon ground cinnamon
¼ teaspoon ground cloves
½ cup (1 stick) butter, at room temperature
½ cup sugar
1 egg, at room temperature
¾ cup molasses
whipped cream, for serving
chopped stem ginger, for decorating

1 ▲ Preheat the oven to 350°F. Line the bottom of an 8-inch square cake pan with wax paper and grease the paper and sides of the pan.

2 ▲ Add the vinegar to the milk and set aside. It will curdle.

3 In another mixing bowl, sift all the dry ingredients together 3 times and set aside.

4 With an electric mixer, cream the butter and sugar until light and fluffy. Beat in the egg until well combined.

5 ▼ Stir in the molasses.

6 ▲ Fold in the dry ingredients in 4 batches, alternating with the curdled milk. Mix only enough to blend.

7 Pour into the prepared pan and bake until firm, 45–50 minutes. Cut into squares and serve warm, with whipped cream. Decorate with the stem ginger.

Classic Cheesecake

SERVES 8

½ cup graham cracker crumbs

2 pounds cream cheese, at room temperature

1¼ cups sugar

grated rind of 1 lemon

3 tablespoons fresh lemon juice

1 teapoon vanilla extract

4 eggs, at room temperature

1 Preheat the oven to 325°F. Grease an 8-inch springform pan. Place on a round of foil 4–5 inches larger than the diameter of the pan. Press it up the sides to seal tightly.

2 Sprinkle the crumbs in the base of the pan. Press to form an even layer.

3 With an electric mixer, beat the cream cheese until smooth. Add the sugar, lemon rind and juice, and vanilla, and beat until blended. Beat in the eggs, 1 at a time. Beat just enough to blend thoroughly.

4 ▲ Pour into the prepared pan. Set the pan in a larger baking pan and place in the oven. Pour enough hot water in the outer pan to come 1 inch up the side of the pan.

5 Bake until the top of the cake is golden brown, about 1½ hours. Let cool in the pan.

6 ▼ Run a knife around the edge to loosen, then remove the rim of the pan. Refrigerate for at least 4 hours before serving.

Chocolate Cheesecake

SERVES 10–12

6 1-ounce squares semisweet chocolate

4 1-ounce squares unsweetened chocolate

2½ pounds cream cheese, at room temperature

1 cup sugar

2 teaspoons vanilla extract

4 eggs, at room temperature

¾ cup sour cream

FOR THE CRUST

1½ cups chocolate wafer crumbs

6 tablespoons butter, melted

½ teaspoon ground cinnamon

1 Preheat the oven to 350°F. Grease the bottom and sides of a 9- × 3-inch springform pan.

2 ▲ For the crust, mix the chocolate crumbs with the butter and cinnamon. Press evenly in the bottom of the pan.

3 Melt both chocolates in the top of a double boiler, or in a heatproof bowl set over hot water. Set aside.

4 With an electric mixer, beat the cream cheese until smooth, then beat in the sugar and vanilla. Add the eggs, 1 at a time, scraping the bowl with a spatula when necessary.

5 Add the sour cream. Stir in the melted chocolate.

6 ▼ Pour into the crust. Bake for 1 hour. Let cool in the pan; remove rim. Refrigerate before serving.

Classic Cheesecake (top), Chocolate Cheesecake

Lemon Mousse Cheesecake

SERVES 10–12

2½ pounds cream cheese, at room temperature

1½ cups sugar

⅓ cup flour

4 eggs, at room temperature, separated

½ cup fresh lemon juice

grated rind of 2 lemons

1 cup graham cracker crumbs

1 Preheat the oven to 325°F. Line a 10- × 2-inch round cake pan with wax paper and grease.

2 With an electric mixer, beat the cream cheese until smooth. Gradually add 1¼ cups of the sugar, and beat until light. Beat in the flour.

3 ▲ Add the egg yolks, and lemon juice and rind, and beat until smooth and well blended.

4 In another bowl, beat the egg whites until they hold soft peaks. Add the remaining sugar and beat until stiff and glossy.

5 ▲ Add the egg whites to the cheese mixture and gently fold in.

6 Pour the batter into the prepared pan, then place the pan in a larger baking pan. Place in the oven and pour hot water in the outer pan to come 1 inch up the side.

7 Bake until golden, 60–65 minutes. Let cool in the pan on a rack. Cover and refrigerate for at least 4 hours.

8 To unmold, run a knife around the inside edge. Place a flat plate, bottom-side up, over the pan and invert onto the plate. Smooth the top with a metal spatula.

9 ▲ Sprinkle the crumbs over the top in an even layer, pressing down slightly to make a top crust.

10 To serve, cut slices with a sharp knife dipped in hot water.

Marbled Cheesecake

SERVES 10

½ cup unsweetened cocoa powder
5 tablespoons hot water
2 pounds cream cheese, at room temperature
1 cup sugar
4 eggs
1 teaspoon vanilla extract
½ cup graham cracker crumbs

1 Preheat the oven to 350°F. Line an 8- × 3-inch cake pan with wax paper and grease.

2 Sift the cocoa powder into a bowl. Pour over the hot water and stir to dissolve. Set aside.

3 With an electric mixer, beat the cheese until smooth and creamy. Add the sugar and beat to incorporate. Beat in the eggs, one at a time. Do not overmix.

4 Divide the mixture evenly between 2 bowls. Stir the chocolate mixture into one, then add the vanilla to the remaining mixture.

5 ▲ Pour a cupful of the plain mixture into the center of the pan; it will spread out into an even layer. Slowly pour over a cupful of chocolate mixture in the center.

6 ▲ Repeat alternating cupfuls of the batters in a circular pattern until both are used up.

7 Set the cake pan in a larger baking pan and pour in hot water to come 1½ inches up the sides of the cake pan.

8 Bake until the top of the cake is golden, about 1½ hours. It will rise during baking but will sink later. Let cool in the pan on a rack.

9 To unmold, run a knife around the inside edge. Place a flat plate, bottom-side up, over the pan and invert onto the plate.

10 ▼ Sprinkle the crumbs evenly over the base, gently place another plate over the crumbs, and invert again. Cover and refrigerate for at least 3 hours, or overnight. To serve, cut slices with a sharp knife dipped in hot water.

Heart Cake

MAKES 1 CAKE

1 cup (2 sticks) butter or margarine, at room temperature

1 cup sugar

4 eggs, at room temperature

1½ cups flour

1 teaspoon baking powder

½ teaspoon baking soda

2 tablespoons milk

1 teaspoon vanilla extract

FOR FROSTING AND DECORATING

3 egg whites

1½ cups granulated sugar

2 tablespoons cold water

2 tablespoons fresh lemon juice

¼ teaspoon cream of tartar

pink food coloring

¾–1 cup confectioners' sugar

1 Preheat the oven to 350°F. Line an 8-inch heart-shaped cake pan with wax paper and grease.

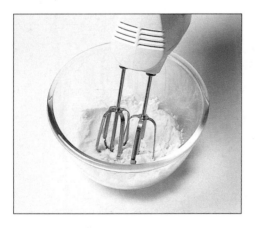

2 ▲ With an electric mixer, cream the butter or margarine and sugar until light and fluffy. Add the eggs, 1 at a time, beating thoroughly after each addition.

3 Sift the flour, baking powder, and baking soda together. Fold the dry ingredients into the butter mixture in 3 batches, alternating with the milk. Stir in the vanilla.

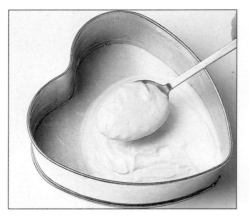

4 ▲ Spoon the batter into the prepared pan and bake until a cake tester inserted in the center comes out clean, 35–40 minutes. Let the cake stand in the pan for 5 minutes, then unmold and transfer to a rack to cool completely.

5 For the frosting, combine 2 of the egg whites, the granulated sugar, water, lemon juice, and cream of tartar in the top of a double boiler or in a bowl set over simmering water. With an electric mixer, beat until thick and holds soft peaks, about 7 minutes. Remove from the heat and continue beating until the mixture is thick enough to spread. Tint the frosting with the pink food coloring.

6 ▲ Put the cake on a board, about 12 inches square, covered in foil or in paper suitable for contact with food. Spread the frosting evenly on the cake. Smooth the top and sides. Leave to set 3–4 hours, or overnight.

7 ▲ For the paper piping bags, fold an 11- × 8-inch sheet of parchment or wax paper in half diagonally, then cut into 2 pieces along the fold mark. Roll over the short side, so that it meets the right-angled corner and forms a cone. To form the piping bag, hold the cone in place with one hand, wrap the point of the long side of the triangle around the cone, and tuck inside, folding over twice to secure. Snip a hole in the pointed end and slip in a small metal piping tip to extend about ¼ inch.

8 For the piped decorations, place 1 tablespoon of the remaining egg white in a bowl and whisk until frothy. Gradually beat in enough confectioners' sugar to make a stiff mixture suitable for piping.

9 ▲ Spoon into a paper piping bag to half-fill. Fold over the top and squeeze to pipe decorations on the top and sides of the cake.

Cup Cakes

MAKES 16

½ cup (1 stick) butter, at room temperature
1 cup granulated sugar
2 eggs, at room temperature
1½ cups cake flour
¼ teaspoon salt
1½ teaspoons baking powder
½ cup plus 1 tablespoon milk
1 teaspoon vanilla extract
FOR FROSTING AND DECORATING
2 large egg whites
3½ cups sifted confectioners' sugar
1–2 drops glycerin
juice of 1 lemon
food colorings
colored sprinkles, for decorating
candied lemon and orange slices, for decorating

1 Preheat the oven to 375°F.

2 ▲ Fill 16 muffin cups with fluted paper baking liners, or grease.

~ COOK'S TIP ~

Ready-made cake decorating products are widely available, and may be used, if preferred, instead of the recipes given for frosting and decorating. Colored gel in tubes with piping tips is useful.

3 With an electric mixer, cream the butter and sugar until light and fluffy. Add the eggs, 1 at a time, beating well after each addition.

4 Sift together the flour, salt, and baking powder. Stir into the butter mixture, alternating with the milk. Stir in the vanilla.

5 ▲ Fill the cups half-full and bake until the tops spring back when touched lightly, about 20 minutes. Let the cup cakes stand in the pan for 5 minutes, then unmold and transfer to a rack to cool completely.

6 For the meringue frosting, beat the egg whites until stiff but not dry. Gradually add the sugar, glycerin, and lemon juice, and continue beating for 1 minute. The consistency should be spreadable. If necessary, thin with a little water or add more sifted confectioners' sugar.

7 ▲ Divide the frosting between several bowls and tint with food colorings. Spread different colored frostings over the cooled cup cakes.

8 ▲ Decorate the cup cakes as wished, such as with different colored sprinkles.

9 ▲ Other decorations include candied orange and lemon slices. Cut into small pieces and arrange on top of the cup cakes. Alternatively, use other suitable candies.

10 ▲ To decorate with colored frostings, fill paper piping bags with different colored frostings. Pipe on faces, or make other designs.

Snake Cake

SERVES 10–12

1 cup (2 sticks) butter or margarine, at room temperature
grated rind and juice of 1 small orange
1 cup granulated sugar
4 eggs, at room temperature, separated
1½ cups flour
1 teaspoon baking powder
⅛ teaspoon salt
FOR FROSTING AND DECORATING
2 tablespoons unsalted butter, at room temperature
3 cups confectioners' sugar
5 1-ounce squares semisweet chocolate
⅛ teaspoon salt
½ cup sour cream
1 egg white
green and blue food colorings

1 Preheat the oven to 375°F. Grease 2 8½-inch ring molds and dust them with flour.

2 With an electric mixer, cream the butter or margarine, orange rind, and sugar until light and fluffy. Beat in the egg yolks, 1 at a time.

3 Sift the flour and baking powder. Fold the flour into the butter mixture, alternating with the orange juice.

4 ▲ In another bowl, beat the egg whites and salt until stiff.

5 Fold a large dollop of the egg whites into the creamed butter mixture to lighten it, then gently fold in the remaining whites.

6 Divide the batter between the prepared pans and bake until a cake tester inserted in the center comes out clean, about 25 minutes. Let stand 5 minutes, then unmold and transfer to a rack to cool.

7 Prepare a board, about 24 × 8 inches, covered in paper suitable for contact with food, or in foil.

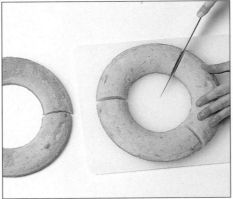

8 ▲ Cut the cakes in 3 even pieces. Trim to level the flat side, if necessary, and shape the head by cutting off wedges from the front. Shape the tail in the same way.

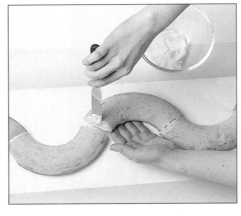

9 ▲ For the butter frosting, mix the butter and ⅓ cup of the confectioners' sugar. Use to join the cake segments and arrange on the board.

10 ▲ For the chocolate frosting, melt the chocolate. Stir in the salt and sour cream. When cool, spread over the cake and smooth the surface.

11 ▲ For decorating, beat the egg white until frothy. Add enough of the remaining confectioners' sugar to obtain a thick mixture. Divide among several bowls and add food colorings.

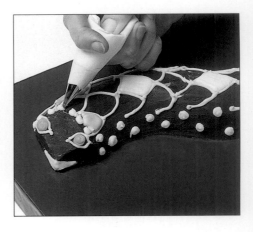

12 ▲ Fill paper piping bags with frosting and pipe decorations.

Sun Cake

SERVES 10–12

½ cup (1 stick) unsalted butter
6 eggs
1 cup sugar
1 cup cake flour
½ teaspoon salt
1 teaspoon vanilla extract

FOR FROSTING AND DECORATING

2 tablespoons unsalted butter, at room temperature
4 cups sifted confectioners' sugar
½ cup apricot jam
2 tablespoons water
2 large egg whites
1–2 drops glycerin
juice of 1 lemon
yellow and orange food colorings

1 Preheat the oven to 350°F. Line 2 8- × 2-inch round cake pans, then grease and flour.

2 In a saucepan, melt the butter over very low heat. Skim off any foam that rises to the surface, then set aside.

3 ▲ Place a heatproof bowl over a saucepan of hot water. Add the eggs and sugar. Beat with an electric mixer until the mixture doubles in volume and is thick enough to leave a ribbon trail when the beaters are lifted, 8–10 minutes.

4 Sift the flour and salt together 3 times. Sift over the egg mixture in 3 batches, folding in well after each addition. Fold in the melted butter and vanilla.

5 Divide the batter between the pans. Level the surfaces and bake until the cakes shrink slightly from the sides of the pans, 25–30 minutes. Let stand 5 minutes, then unmold and transfer to a cooling rack.

6 Prepare a board, about 16 inches square, covered in paper suitable for contact with food, or in foil.

7 ▲ For the sunbeams, cut one of the cakes into 8 equal wedges. Cut away a rounded piece from the base of each so that they fit neatly up against the sides of the whole cake.

8 ▲ For the butter frosting, mix the butter and ⅓ cup of the confectioners' sugar. Use to attach the sunbeams.

9 ▲ Melt the jam with the water and brush over the cake. Place on the board and straighten, if necessary.

10 ▲ For the frosting, beat the egg whites until stiff but not dry. Gradually add 3½ cups of the sugar, the glycerin, and lemon juice, and continue beating for 1 minute. The consistency should be spreadable. If necessary, thin with water or add more sugar. Tint with yellow food coloring and spread over the cake.

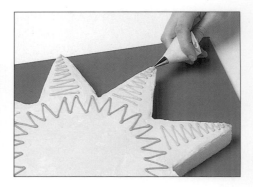

11 ▲ Divide the remaining frosting in half and tint with more food coloring to obtain bright yellow and orange. Pipe decorative zig-zags on the sunbeams and a face in the middle.

Jack-O'-Lantern Cake

SERVES 8–10

1½ cups cake flour
2½ teaspoons baking powder
⅛ teaspoon salt
½ cup (1 stick) butter, at room temperature
1 cup granulated sugar
3 egg yolks, at room temperature, well beaten
1 teaspoon grated lemon rind
¾ cup milk
FOR THE CAKE COVERING
5–6 cups confectioners' sugar
2 egg whites
2 tablespoons liquid glucose
orange and black food colorings

1 Preheat the oven to 375°F. Line an 8-inch round cake pan with wax paper and grease.

2 Sift together the flour, baking powder, and salt. Set aside.

3 With an electric mixer, cream the butter and sugar until light and fluffy. Gradually beat in the egg yolks, then add the lemon rind. Fold in the flour mixture in 3 batches, alternating with the milk.

4 Spoon the batter into the prepared pan. Bake until a cake tester inserted in the center comes out clean, about 35 minutes. Let stand 5 minutes, then unmold and transfer to a rack.

~ **COOK'S TIP** ~

If preferred, use ready-made roll-out cake covering or rolled fondant, available at specialist cake decorating supply shops and some supermarkets. Knead in food coloring, if required.

5 For the covering, sift 4½ cups of the confectioners' sugar into a bowl. Make a well in the center, add 1 egg white, the glucose, and orange food coloring. Stir until a dough forms.

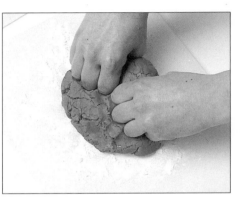

6 ▲ Transfer to a work surface dusted with confectioners' sugar and knead briefly.

7 ▲ Roll out the cake covering to a sheet about ⅛ inch thick.

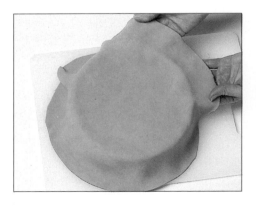

8 ▲ Gently place the sheet on top of the cooled cake and smooth the sides. Trim the excess and reserve.

9 ▲ From the trimmings, cut shapes for the lid. Tint the remaining cake covering trimmings with black food coloring. Roll out thinly and cut shapes for the face.

10 ▲ Brush the undersides with water and arrange the face and lid on the cake.

11 ▲ Place 1 tablespoon of the remaining egg white in a bowl and stir in enough confectioners' sugar to make a thick frosting. Tint with black food coloring, fill a paper piping bag, and pipe the outline of the lid.

Stars and Stripes Cake

1 cup (2 sticks) butter or margarine, at room temperature

1 cup dark brown sugar, firmly packed

1 cup granulated sugar

5 eggs, at room temperature

2½ cups flour

2 teaspoons baking powder

1 teaspoon baking soda

1 teaspoon ground cinnamon

1 teaspoon ground ginger

½ teaspoon ground allspice

¼ teaspoon ground cloves

¼ teaspoon salt

1½ cups buttermilk

½ cup raisins

FOR THE CAKE COVERING

2 tablespoons butter

9-10½ cups confectioners' sugar

3 egg whites

4 tablespoons liquid glucose

red and blue food colorings

---

1 Preheat the oven to 350°F. Line a 9- × 12-inch baking pan with wax paper and grease.

2 With an electric mixer, cream the butter or margarine and sugars until light and fluffy. Gradually beat in the eggs, one at a time, beating well after each addition.

3 Sift together the flour, baking powder, baking soda, spices, and salt. Fold into the butter mixture in 3 batches, alternating with the buttermilk. Stir in the raisins.

4 Pour the batter into the prepared pan and bake until the cake springs back when touched lightly, about 35 minutes. Let stand 10 minutes, then unmold and transfer to a rack.

5 For assembly, make the butter frosting. Mix the butter with ⅓ cup of the confectioners' sugar.

6 ▲ When the cake is cool, cut a curved shape from the top.

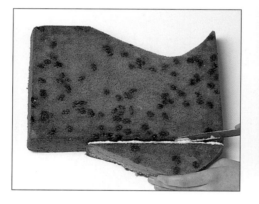

7 ▲ Attach it to the bottom of the cake with the butter frosting.

8 Prepare a board, about 16 × 12 inches, covered in paper suitable for contact with food, or in foil. Transfer the cake to the board.

9 For the cake covering, sift 9 cups of the confectioners' sugar into a bowl. Add 2 of the egg whites and the liquid glucose. Stir until the mixture forms a dough.

10 Cover and set aside half of the covering. On a work surface dusted with confectioners' sugar, roll out the remaining covering to a sheet. Transfer to the cake. Smooth the sides and trim any excess.

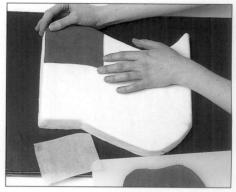

11 ▲ Tint one-quarter of the remaining covering blue and tint the rest red. Roll out the blue to a thin sheet and cut out the background for the stars. Place on the cake.

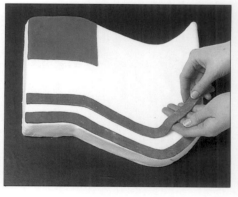

12 ▲ Roll out the red covering, cut out stripes, and place on the cake.

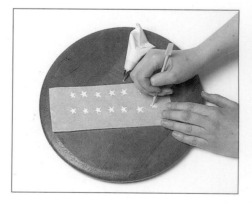

13 ▲ For the stars, mix 1 tablespoon of the egg white with just enough confectioners' sugar to thicken. Pipe small stars on to a sheet of wax paper and leave to set. When dry, peel them off and place on the blue background.

Index

~